quick and easy
party cakes

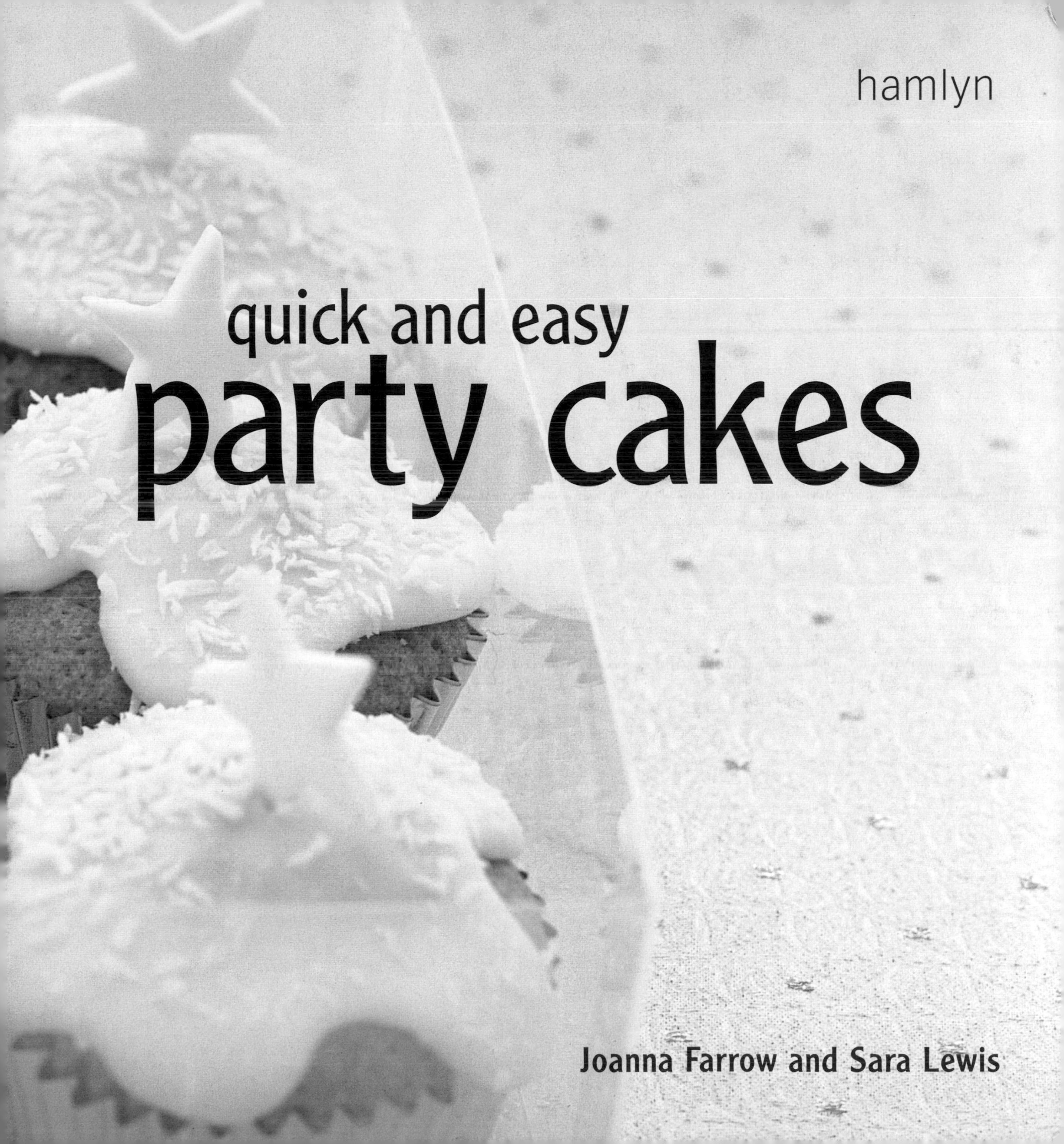

hamlyn

quick and easy
party cakes

Joanna Farrow and Sara Lewis

First published in Great Britain in 2006 by Hamlyn,
a division of Octopus Publishing Group Ltd
2–4 Heron Quays
London E14 4JP

Copyright © Octopus Publishing Group 2006

Distributed in the United States and Canada by Sterling Publishing Co., Inc.
387 Park Avenue South, New York, NY 10016–8810

ISBN-13: 978-0-600-61565-1
ISBN-10: 0-600-61565-0

A CIP catalogue record for this book is available from the British Library

Printed and bound in China

10 9 8 7 6 5 4 3 2 1

contents

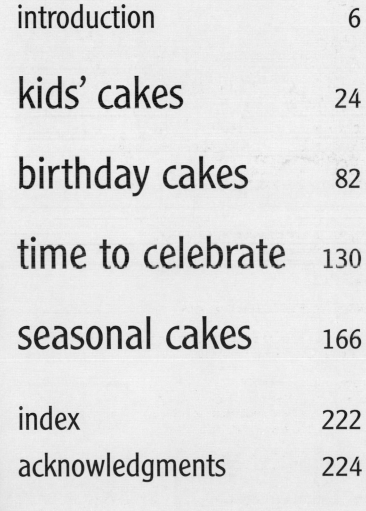

introduction

Nothing completes a party quite like a wonderful homemade cake. It adds a personal touch to any celebration, and, whether it's a birthday, anniversary, graduation, or wedding, a lovingly prepared cake that's been personalized for the occasion will be enjoyed and appreciated by all.

Many people avoid making their own cakes and resort to bought varieties instead because they lack the confidence and skills required to make a cake from scratch. With the help of this book, you'll soon realize that baking, frosting, and decorating your own party cakes is surprisingly easy, as well as being an extremely rewarding experience. If you're short of time, a store-bought base can be quickly transformed into a fabulous party cake with one of the many ideas in the following chapters.

Once you've mastered the basics you'll be creating more adventurous cakes in no time at all, and you'll soon be taking a cake along with you to every party. We'll take you through some basic

cake recipes, as well as providing information on frosting and decorating, there are also some top tips to ensure you get great results every time. The recipes cover every imaginable type of party and celebration, and they've all been selected because they don't require any specialized skills. So, even if you've never baked a cake before, you can try your hand at easy but impressive cakes for a children's party, such as the Chocolate Hedgehogs (page 74), or more sophisticated cakes for special occasions, such as a Winter Wedding Cake (page 144). Baking your own party cakes is a rewarding experience and you can be absolutely sure that your friends and family will thank you for it, too!

essential equipment

The recipes in this book are all easy to make, and you shouldn't really require a lot of specialized equipment. You'll probably find that you already have a lot of things in your kitchen, but, if you do need to buy anything extra, it's probably best to visit a specialty cake-decorating store. This is the best place to go for specialized equipment, such as cutters in all shapes and sizes, as well as for ready-made cake decorations, icing, and food colorings. Many companies also offer a mail order service if you don't have a local store, and, of course, you'll find plenty of ordering services on the Internet.

Here we have listed some of the basic equipment and utensils that you'll need for many of the recipes—this should be plenty to get you going.

- **Large and small spatulas (essential for spreading frosting)**
- **Kitchen scale**
- **Rolling pin**
- **Pastry brush**
- **Scissors**
- **Selection of bowls in various sizes**
- **Sifter/strainer**
- **Cake pans (at least one round and one square, with loose bases)**
- **Muffin pans (for cupcakes)**
- **Baking pans**
- **Waxed and nonstick parchment paper**
- **Cookie sheets**
- **Whisk**

basic cake recipes

With many of the recipes in this book you have the option either to use a store-bought cake as the base or to make your own. Because it's so easy to make the actual cake yourself, it's always better to do so. Although, if you're short of time, store-bought cakes are perfectly acceptable, though they tend to be quite small and shallow. If you make your own cake, you have complete control over the size and type of cake that you use, and the end result will be far superior, as well as cheaper. Why not make a big batch of cakes at one time and then freeze them until you're ready to complete them with frosting and decorations? On the following pages there are a selection of basic cake recipes that are easy to make, and you will also find some quick variations.

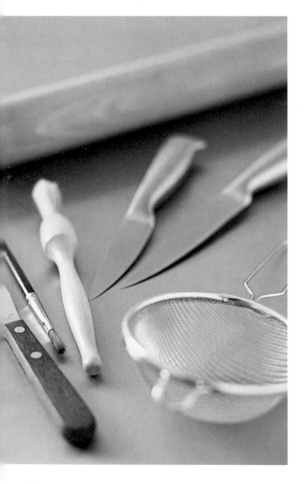

basic sponge cake

square cake	5 inch	6 inch	7 inch	8 inch	9 inch
round cake	6 inch	7 inch	8 inch	9 inch	10 inch
serves	8	12	16	20	24
cooking time	40 minutes	50–60 minutes	1 hour	1–1¼ hours	1¼–1½ hours

ingredients

unsalted butter, softened	¾ cup	1 cup	1⅓ cups	1½ cups	2 cups
superfine sugar	¾ cup	1 cup	1⅓ cups	1½ cups	2 cups
medium eggs	3	4	5	6	8
milk	2 tablespoons	3 tablespoons	4 tablespoons	5 tablespoons	⅔ cup
self-rising flour	2 cups	2½ cups	3¼ cups	5 cups	6 cups

flavor variations

vanilla					
vanilla extract	1 teaspoon	2 teaspoons	1 tablespoon	4 teaspoons	2 tablespoons
orange or lemon					
substitute juice for milk					
orange or lemon zest	zest of 1	zest of 1	zest of 1½	zest of 2	zest of 3
orange or lemon juice	2 tablespoons	3 tablespoons	4 tablespoons	5 tablespoons	⅔ cup
chocolate					
substitute cocoa powder for equal amount of flour					
cocoa powder	¼ cup	⅓ cup	½ cup	⅔ cup	¾ cup

1 Use a wooden spoon or electric beater to cream the butter and sugar together until light and fluffy. Lightly beat the eggs with the milk in a separate bowl. Gradually beat the eggs and milk into the creamed mixture, alternating with the flour.

2 Turn the mixture into the prepared pan (see page 19) and level the surface. Bake in a preheated oven, 325°F, for the time indicated in the chart or until a tester, inserted in the center, comes out clean. Leave the cake in the pan for 10 minutes, then transfer it to a wire rack to cool.

rich chocolate cake

square cake	5 inch	7 inch	9 inch
round cake	6 inch	8 inch	10 inch
serves	10	18	24
cooking time	1 hour	1¼ hours	1½ hours
ingredients			
cocoa powder	¾ cup	1 cup	1½ cups
boiling water	1 cup	1½ cups	2¼ cups
unsalted butter, softened	½ cup	1 cup	1½ cups
light brown sugar	1½ cups	2 cups	3½ cups
eggs, beaten	2	3	5
all-purpose flour	1¾ cups	2½ cups	4 cups
baking powder	1 teaspoon	1½ teaspoons	2½ teaspoons

1 Put the cocoa powder in a bowl and gradually beat in the boiling water until smooth. Allow to cool.

2 Beat together the butter and sugar until they are creamy. Gradually beat in the eggs, a little at a time, adding a little of the flour to prevent curdling. Sift the remaining flour over the bowl with the baking powder. Use a large metal spoon to fold in the flour. Stir in the cocoa mixture.

3 Turn the mixture into the prepared pan (see page 19). Bake in a preheated oven, 350°F, for the time stated in the chart or until the crust is just firm. For a good, moist texture the center of the cake should have a slight wobble when it comes out of the oven.

4 Allow to cool in the pan, then wrap and store for up to 3 days in a cool place or freeze.

rich fruit cake

square cake	5 inch	7 inch	9 inch
round cake	6 inch	8 inch	10 inch
serves	14	24	40
cooking time	2–2½ hours	3½–3¾ hours	4–4½ hours
ingredients			
unsalted butter, softened	⅔ cup	1 cup	1¾ cups
light brown sugar	¾ cups	1¼ cups	2¼ cups
eggs, beaten	3	5	8
all-purpose flour	1¾ cups	2¾ cups	5 cups
ground mixed spice	2 teaspoons	1 tablespoon	2 tablespoons
preserved ginger, chopped	1½ pieces	2 pieces	3½ pieces
luxury mixed dried fruit	4 cups	6⅔ cups	13⅓ cups
blanched chopped almonds	¼ cup	⅔ cup	1 cup

1 Beat together the butter and sugar until creamy. Gradually beat in the eggs, a little at a time, adding a little of the flour if the mixture starts to curdle.

2 Sift the flour with the spice and stir into the mixture. Add the ginger, dried fruit, and almonds and stir the ingredients until they are evenly combined.

3 Turn the mixture into the prepared pan (see page 19) and level the surface. Bake in a preheated oven, 275°F, for the time indicated in the chart or until a tester, inserted into the center, comes out clean. Allow to cool in the pan.

4 Remove the cake from the pan and wrap it in foil. If necessary, you can store it for up to 6 months in a cool, dry place until you are ready to frost it.

jelly roll

serves 10
cooking time 10–12 minutes

ingredients

3 large eggs
½ cup superfine sugar, plus extra
  for dusting
1 cup self-rising flour
6–8 tablespoons raspberry
  or strawberry jelly

1 Grease and line a jelly roll pan, 13 x 9 inches. Put the eggs and sugar in a heatproof bowl over a pan of gently simmering water and beat until light and airy and the beater leaves a trail when lifted. Remove from the heat and beat for a further 3 minutes.

2 Sift the flour over the bowl and use a large metal spoon to fold it in, adding 1 tablespoon of hot water once most of the flour is incorporated. Turn the mixture into the pan and spread it into the corners. Bake in a preheated oven, 400°F, for 10–12 minutes until just firm to the touch.

3 Meanwhile, sprinkle a sheet of waxed paper with superfine sugar. Turn the warm cake out onto the paper and spread it with the jelly. Starting from a short end, roll up the cake. Place it seam-side down on a wire rack to cool.

chocolate jelly roll

serves 10
cooking time 10–12 minutes

ingredients

3 large eggs
⅓ cup superfine sugar, plus extra
  for dusting
½ cup self-rising flour
¼ cup cocoa powder, sifted
1¼ cups heavy or whipping cream
  or 6–8 tablespoons jelly

1 Make the cake as above, adding the cocoa powder with the flour in step 2.

2 Spread the warm cake with jelly or with whipped cream before rolling it up.

cupcakes

makes 12
cooking time 18–20 minutes

ingredients

⅔ cup unsalted butter, softened
⅔ cup superfine sugar
1½ cups self-rising flour
3 eggs
2 teaspoons vanilla extract

1 Line a 12-section muffin pan with paper bake cups. Put all the ingredients in a bowl and beat with a hand-held electric beater for 1–2 minutes until the mixture is light and creamy. Divide the mixture among the cups.

2 Bake the cakes in a preheated oven, 350°F, for 18–20 minutes until they are risen and just firm to the touch. Transfer the cakes to a wire rack to cool.

choux pastry buns

makes 40

cooking time 23–25 minutes

ingredients

1 cup all-purpose flour
½ cup unsalted butter,
   cut into pieces
4 eggs, beaten

1 Sift the flour onto a piece of paper. Melt the butter in a medium saucepan with 1¼ cups water. Bring to a boil and tip the flour into the saucepan. Beat with a wooden spoon over the heat for about 1 minute or until the mixture forms a ball in the center of the pan. Allos to cool for 2 minutes.

2 Gradually beat in the eggs, a little at a time, until the paste is smooth and glossy. Using 2 teaspoons, place spoonfuls of the paste on cookie sheets, spacing them about 2 inches apart. You should have enough mixture for about 40 small spoonfuls.

3 Bake the buns in a preheated oven, 425°F, for about 20 minutes until they are risen and golden. Remove from the oven and make a slit in the side of each bun to allow the steam to escape. Return them to the oven for an additional 3–5 minutes until firm. Transfer to a wire rack to cool.

the icing on the cake

Many people find that frosting and decorating their cakes is the most enjoyable part. There are so many options available that it really depends on the type of cake you've prepared and the nature of the celebration as to which type of icing you choose. The recipes in this book require many different kinds of icing—this section shows some of the most widely used.

buttercream

quantity	single	double	triple	quadruple
butter, softened	⅓ cup	⅔ cup	1 cup	1¼ cup
confectioners' sugar	1 cup	2 cups	3 cups	4 cups
hot water	1 teaspoon	2 teaspoons	3 teaspoons	4 teaspoons
flavor variations				
vanilla extract	½ teaspoon	1 teaspoon	1½ teaspoons	2 teaspoons
citrus zest (use fruit juice instead of hot water)	2 teaspoons	4 teaspoons	6 teaspoons	8 teaspoons
coffee granules dissolved in hot water	1 teaspoon in 1 teaspoon water	2 teaspoons in 1 tablespoon water	3 teaspoons in 1 tablespoon water	4 teaspoons in 2 tablespoons water

Buttercream (or butter frosting), which is simply made by blending together confectioners' sugar and butter, has a delicious flavor and excellent texture, and it is extremely versatile. For the best flavor use a good quality, unsalted butter and beat it thoroughly with the sugar so it's easy to apply. Spread the cake with a thin layer of the buttercream to stick the crumbs in place, which will make a manageable base for the rest of the buttercream. Freshly packed confectioners' sugar is usually fine to use straight from the package, but if you open it and it looks a bit lumpy, sift it first. If you want to flavor your buttercream, choose from one of the flavorings above and beat the ingredients into the buttercream once it's made. Remember that coffee will alter the color of the buttercream, so bear this in mind if you're using it as a covering rather than as a filling.

1 Beat together the butter and a little of the confectioners' sugar in a bowl until smooth.

2 Gradually beat in the remaining sugar and hot water until pale and creamy.

Glacé icing

Basic glacé icing is made by beating together confectioners' sugar and water into a smooth paste. It really is that easy, but you'll probably want a little practice before you move on to variations. There are lots of alternative recipes that you can try, either to incorporate the flavors of the cake or to add subtle variations. For example, you can use orange or lemon juice instead of water or add other flavorings such as instant coffee or chocolate powder. If you want to include some color in your icing, add a dash of food coloring. Use a thin glacé icing to coat the top of cakes, or you can add extra confectioners' sugar for a stiffer consistency and then use this for decorative piping.

Rolled fondant

This is a ready-to-use commercial icing that's available from some supermarkets or specialty cake stores. It generally comes in white but, like the other icings, you can easily adapt the color and flavor to suit your needs by kneading it with food coloring or flavoring extracts. Fondant is extremely adaptable and you can either roll it out and cut it into shapes or use it to create novelty decorations to put on top of cakes. Rolled fondant has to be kneaded before use to warm it up and make it more pliable. Dust your work surface with confectioners' sugar when you're working with the fondant to stop it sticking—otherwise it can be very messy to work with.

Decorator frosting

This is another ready-to-use commercial icing that comes in tubes with a variety of tips for piping. It's also available in a range of different colors. It's great for birthday cakes in particular because you can easily write names and ages on top of your cake.

Ganache

Ganache is one of the most luxurious of all the icings, a pure blend of chocolate and cream. Once made, it'll need 15–30 minutes to thicken up before use, but keep an eye on it because it will gradually become too thick to use so you need to be ready when it's exactly the right consistency. This quantity makes enough to cover an 8 inch round cake.

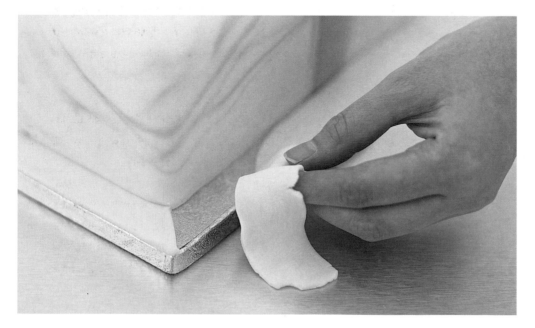

dark chocolate ganache

makes enough to cover an 8 inch round cake

ingredients

- 1¼ cups heavy cream
- 10 oz good quality dark chocolate, chopped

1 Heat the cream in a medium, heavy saucepan until it is bubbling around the edge. Remove from the heat and stir in the chopped chocolate.

2 Allow to stand until the chocolate has melted. Turn the mixture into a bowl and chill until the ganache is cool enough to hold its shape. The cooling time will depend on the temperature to which the cream is heated. As a guide, check after about 15 minutes, although it might take 30–40 minutes.

white chocolate ganache

makes enough to cover an 8 inch round cake

ingredients

- 1¼ cups heavy cream
- 10 oz good quality white chocolate, chopped

1 Heat half the cream in a medium, heavy saucepan until it is bubbling around the edge. Remove from the heat and stir in the chocolate.

2 Allow to stand until the chocolate has melted. Turn the mixture into a bowl and chill for about 15 minutes until cold.

3 Stir in the remaining cream and beat with a hand-held electric beater until the ganache just holds its shape. Don't over-beat the mixture or the cream will start to curdle.

chocolate fudge frosting

This frosting develops a fudge-like consistency when set, making a delicious filling and covering for chocolate or sponge cakes. It thickens as it cools, so make sure you use it while it is spreadable. If it does solidify before you've had a chance to use it, simply beat in a dash of hot water. It's an easy recipe to double up on quantities if you've made a larger cake.

makes enough to cover an 8 inch round cake

ingredients

2 tablespoons unsalted butter
2 tablespoons cocoa powder
1½ cups confectioners' sugar
2 tablespoons milk

1 Melt the butter in a small saucepan. Stir in the cocoa powder and cook, stirring constantly, for 30 seconds until smooth. Remove the pan from the heat and gradually stir in the confectioners' sugar (no need to sift) and milk, mixing until smooth.

2 Return the pan to the heat for 1 minute, stirring constantly, until the frosting has a glossy pouring consistency. Quickly spread the frosting over the cake while it is still warm.

royal icing

Royal icing hardens once it dries out. To compensate for this, if you're making a wedding or Christmas cake well in advance, beat in a teaspoon of glycerin. If you're not using the icing immediately, press a sheet of plastic wrap directly over the surface of the icing to prevent a crust forming.

makes enough to cover an 8 inch round cake

ingredients

2 egg whites
4 cups confectioners' sugar

1 Using a hand-held electric beater, beat the egg whites in a large bowl with a little of the confectioners' sugar until smooth.

2 Gradually beat in the remaining confectioners' sugar until the icing is softly peaking. You might not need all the sugar.

techniques and tips

There are a number of techniques that are good to know if you're planning to make a lot of party cakes. You'll find all these useful for the recipes in this book.

Lining a round cake pan

Using the pan as a guide, draw a circle on waxed paper and cut it out. Cut strips of paper a little wider than the height of the pan, fold over a lip about ½ inch wide and snip it at intervals. Fit the paper around the sides of the pan so the lip sits flat on the base. If you need more than one strip of paper to go round the sides, overlap them slightly. Press the circle into the base and brush all the paper with melted butter or margarine.

Lining a square cake pan

This technique is similar to the one above, but once you've cut the square base and strips, you only need to make snips in the paper at the corners to make sure it fits squarely into the corners of the pan. Brush the paper with a little melted butter or margarine. For shallower pans, such as roasting pans, simply snip into the corners of a large piece of greased waxed paper and press it into the base of the pan.

Using ready-to-use icing

Soft and pliable, store-bought, ready-to-use icing is easy to use. Large packs of white icing are widely available, and many supermarkets sell smaller packs of icings in basic colors. For a choice of more interesting colors try your local cake-decorating store, where you should find a good range of different shades in handy 8 oz packages. Once the package is opened, the icing will gradually dry out, making it impossible to use. To prevent this, tightly wrap any unused icing in plastic wrap, even if it's just for a short time. Leftover icing can be stored in a cool place for several months or in the freezer. Before using, knead it with a bit of confectioners' sugar to remove any stickiness.

Food colorings

Food colorings are available in several forms. Liquid colors—the type that are often available in supermarkets—tend to be less intense, so you might not be able to reach the shade you want before the icing has become too wet to use. They are useful for pastel shades, however, or for painting onto icing.

Paste colors are much more intense and come in a wider range of colors. The basic ones, including red and black, can be bought from most supermarkets, but for a much wider choice, visit a specialty cake-decorating store.

Powder colors, also available from cake-decorating stores, can be kneaded into icing

but they're usually just dusted onto icing, once the icing is shaped and set. Gold and silver food colors are available in liquid form (just give them a stir before use) or as a powder, which can be mixed to a "paint" with a dash of flavorless cooking oil or a drop of vodka. Some metallic colors aren't edible and should therefore not be applied directly to the cake.

Coloring white icing

Dust your work surface with confectioners' sugar or cornstarch and lightly knead the icing to soften it. Use the tip of a toothpick to dot the icing with paste coloring. A little paste color goes a long way, so add it sparingly at first, particularly if you want a pastel shade. You can always add more later but it's too late if you add too much. If you're adding liquid color use a toothpick or the handle of a teaspoon. Knead the icing until the color is evenly distributed. For a marbled effect, leave the icing streaked with color.

Covering a cake board with icing

Cakes look more sophisticated if you cover the cake board with icing. This can be done either once the cake is iced on the board and only the edges show or, if a lot of the board shows, before the cake is positioned. To cover the whole board, brush the surface of the board with water. Thinly roll out the icing on a surface dusted with confectioners' sugar or cornstarch and lift it over the board. Smooth the icing with the palms of your hands and use a sharp knife to trim off the excess paste around the edges.

To cover the edges of the board, brush the top edge of the board lightly with water. Roll out long, thin strips of the icing trimmings and lay them around the cake, butting a neat cut edge against the cake. Smooth down and trim off the excess around the edges of the board. For a square cake, it's easiest to cover one side of the board at a time. For a round cake, work with the longest strip you can manage, to avoid having too many joins.

Covering a cake with ready-to-use icing

Use a spatula to spread the top and sides of the cake with a thin layer of smooth apricot or red fruit jelly or buttercream. Lightly knead the icing on a surface dusted with confectioners' sugar to soften it slightly and roll it out to a round or square about 5 inches larger in diameter than the cake. Lift the icing over a rolling pin and drape it over the cake. Smooth it over the top of the cake and ease it to fit around the sides. Because icing is so pliable you should be able to shape it around the sides without leaving any creases. Trim off the excess icing. Using the palms of your hands dusted with confectioners' sugar, smooth out any bumps, making the surface as smooth and flat as possible.

Covering a cake with almond paste

Rich fruit cakes are usually covered with a layer of almond paste before being iced. Use

exactly the same technique as for covering a cake with ready-to-use icing. Spread the cake with apricot jelly and then add the almond paste. There's no need to let the almond paste dry out before covering it with either ready-to-use or royal icing.

quantities of almond paste

Square cake	Round cake	Almond paste
5 inch	6 inch	13 oz
7 inch	8 inch	1½ lb
9 inch	10 inch	2½ lb

the finishing touches

This is where a homemade cake really comes into its own. The final decorations will distinguish a wedding cake from a birthday cake and will help to give your cake that personal touch. As tempting as it is, don't overdo the decorations—often the simplest cakes are the most appealing and you don't want to ruin all your hard work by cramming on too many different colors and shapes.

Icing shapes

Ready-to-use icing is easy to use, which makes it perfect for cutting out a variety of shapes. You can either place these directly on the cake or set them aside on a cookie sheet lined with waxed paper or nonstick parchment paper until they have set hard.

Roll out the icing thinly on a surface dusted with confectioners' sugar and cut out the shapes. Dip the cutter or knife in confectioners' sugar first so that it doesn't stick to the icing.

Piped icing

You'll find a variety of tubes of icing in supermarkets or cake stores, but you can make your own paper pastry bag if you prefer. Cut out a 10 inch square of waxed paper or nonstick parchment paper and fold it diagonally in half to make a triangle. Cut along the folded line. Holding the center of the long edge toward you, curl the right-hand point of the triangle over to meet the center point, forming a cone. Bring the left-hand

point over the cone so the 3 points meet. Fold the paper over several times at the points to stop the paper unraveling. Half-fill the bag with your chosen icing and fold up the open end to secure the bag before snipping off the tip. Begin by snipping off a tiny amount to see how finely the mixture flows out. You can then easily snip off a bit more for a wider line of piping if necessary.

Chocolate curls

Run a vegetable peeler along the edge of a chunk of chocolate to make curls. These make a simple but attractive decoration for any number of party cakes and can either be scattered over the cake or else clustered in the center.

Flowers

Fresh flowers look absolutely gorgeous on a cake and are often sufficient in terms of decoration. Add them at the last minute so they remain fresh for as long as possible, or you can wrap the ends of the stems in damp cotton batting and then plastic wrap. Alternatively, you could try using dried or artificial flowers, although fresh flowers will always look much more effective.

Candy

It's a good idea to keep an eye out for any interesting shaped candies when you're out shopping. You can then tuck them away in the pantry until you're baking your next party cake and use them to add an interesting and different twist to the final look of your decorated cake.

Painted decorations

If you like painting and have a steady hand, you'll find painting decorations on the cake with food coloring and a fine artist's paintbrush really rewarding and effective. If there's time, let the icing set first so that it won't dent if you rest your hand on it for support.

1
kids' cakes

ballet shoes

serves 8–10

decoration time 25 minutes

2 x 9 inch bought or homemade
chocolate Jelly Rolls
(see page 12)

3 tablespoons smooth apricot jelly

confectioners' sugar or cornstarch,
for dusting

1 lb pink ready-to-use icing

3 oz white ready-to-use icing

pink decorator frosting or jelly

5 feet pink satin ribbon

1 Use a serrated knife to trim the ends of the jelly rolls into a curve. Scoop an oval, about 5½ x 2 inches and ¾ inch, out of the top of each cake. Brush away any loose crumbs and spread the cakes with the apricot jelly.

2 Dust your work surface with confectioners' sugar or cornstarch and roll out half the pink icing so that it is at least 2 inches larger than a cake all the way around. Lift the icing over the rolling pin and drape it over one of the cakes. Ease it over the sides, smoothing it with your fingertips dusted with cornstarch. Trim off the excess and wrap the trimmings in plastic wrap. Transfer the iced cake to a cookie sheet lined with nonstick parchment paper. Cover the second cake in the same way with the remaining pink icing and transfer it to the cookie sheet.

3 Knead 1 oz of the pink icing trimmings with the white icing, then cut it in half. Roll out one piece to a 6 x 2½ inch oval. Press the oval into one ballet shoe and trim off the excess. Repeat with the remaining icing and the other shoe. Cut thin strips from the trimmings and shape them into bows. Transfer the bows to the cookie sheet to dry.

4 Shape the remaining pink icing into a long rope, then flatten it with a rolling pin to 12 inches long. Cut the strip in half lengthwise and trim the outer edges with a fluted pastry wheel. Brush the top edges of the ballet shoes with water and press the strips around the join where the pale and darker pink icings meet. Add the icing bows, sticking them in place with a little decorator frosting or jelly.

5 Allow the cakes to dry, if you have time, then arrange them in a box lined with patterned tissue paper or on an oval cake board covered with a thin layer of white ready-to-use icing. Decorate with pink satin ribbons.

quick tips

- If you are short of time, put the covered cakes straight onto a cake board and decorate them immediately.

- If you cannot find pink ready-to-use icing you can adapt white icing to suit your needs. Just add drops of red food coloring, a little at a time, until it is the desired shade.

rapunzel

serves 12

decoration time 30 minutes

double quantity pale green Buttercream (see page 15)

11 inch round cake board

3 x 6 inch bought chocolate jelly rolls

2 bought chocolate mini-jelly rolls

confectioners' sugar or cornstarch, for dusting

1½ lb white ready-to-use icing

red paste food coloring

1½ cups mini-marshmallows

1 tube each yellow, black, and red decorator frosting

2 oz yellow ready-to-use icing

1 white chocolate button

1 pink wafer cookie

sugar flowers

candles and candle-holders

1 Thickly spread the buttercream over the cake board. Cut 2 inches off one of the large jelly rolls and stick the cut-off slice onto the top of the second jelly roll with a little buttercream. Thinly spread buttercream over the sides and ends of all the jelly rolls and mini-rolls.

2 Dust your work surface with confectioners' sugar or cornstarch and knead the white ready-to-use icing. Add a little red coloring and knead again until partially mixed, to give a marbled effect. Roll out the icing and cut out rectangles, 8 inches wide and the same length as each roll, to cover all the jelly rolls. Cover the larger jelly roll first and re-roll the trimmings as required.

3 Put the cakes on the board, standing them close together on their ends. Position the mini-rolls at the front with a gap between them for the castle entrance. Roll out the remaining pink icing trimmings and cut out a 2 inch square. Cut a castellated design along one edge, then stick the gate to the mini-rolls with a little buttercream.

4 Decorate the tops of the tower with mini-marshmallows stuck in place with yellow decorator frosting. Add a few marshmallows at the base.

5 Make Rapunzel. Knead the yellow ready-to-use icing and press a small ball into a round. Add the white chocolate button for the face and fold yellow icing hair around the head. Cut the remaining icing in half and shape each piece into 2 long ropes. Twist them together and stick them to the side of the tallest tower with yellow decorator frosting. Draw Rapunzel's eyes and mouth with black and red decorator frosting and stick the head in position. Add tiny pieces of icing at the end of the "plait" to suggest 3 strands.

6 Make the window. Cut the wafer cookie in half and cut a small piece off each end. Stick the larger window pieces to the tower either side of Rapunzel's head and stick one of the shorter pieces of cookie on the castle entrance to make a drawbridge. Add sugar flowers to the cake board and candles in holders to the top of the turrets.

quick tip

- If the castle's entrance droops slightly, prop it up with a piece of folded foil. Remove the foil just before serving.

dolls' house

serves 20

decoration time 30 minutes

5 x 12 oz bought chocolate marble
loaf cakes

12 inch round cake board, plain
or iced

quadruple quantity pink Buttercream
(see page 15)

18 pale pink rectangular iced cookies

4 oz midget gems or other small
fruit gums

8 oz jelly beans

9 pale yellow rectangular
iced cookies

4 pieces pale green fruit rock candy

1 tube yellow decorator frosting

selection of icing flowers

white chocolate buttons

1 Trim the tops and a little off the sides of 4 of the cakes so that they stack together closely on the cake board to make a block 2 cakes wide and 2 cakes high. Sandwich the cakes together with buttercream, then spread a little more on the top. Cut the last cake in half diagonally and butt the halves together to make the roof.

2 Cover the sides and roof of the house thickly with buttercream. Arrange the pink cookies to make the overlapping roof tiles. Arrange the midget gems or fruit gums along the ridge of the roof. Stick the jelly beans under the eaves, down the edges of the house and around the bottom on the cake board.

3 Stick 2 yellow cookies to each side of the house to make windows and another for a door at one end. Use a serrated knife to cut the rock candy in half and press the pieces onto the cake under the windows. Pipe on window bars with yellow icing, then pipe on dots of icing and stick the flowers in place. Attach a midget gem or fruit gum doorknob.

4 Add a few extra flowers to the cake board and use white chocolate buttons to make a path to the front door.

quick tips

• Cover the cake board with 8 oz ready-to-use pale green icing, sticking down the edges with a little apricot jelly. Trim the edges of the icing and allow to harden before placing the cake on top.

• Make an all-chocolate version with white Chocolate Fudge Frosting (see page 18) or vanilla Buttercream (see page 15) with chocolate-covered cookies and candy for decorations.

it's my birthday

serves 6

decoration time 30 minutes

7 inch round bought or homemade Basic Sponge Cake (see page 9)

8 inch square cake board

double quantity pink Buttercream (see page 15)

4 tablespoons strawberry jelly

confectioners' sugar or cornstarch, for dusting

1 lb white ready-to-use icing

1 tube white decorator frosting

2 x 2½ inch thick, non-drip white or pink candles

1 oz package of sugar flowers

1 Using the cake pan as a guide, cut a circle of paper the same size as the sponge cake layers. Fold it into a wedge shape, retaining the curved edge. Using the folded paper as a guide, cut the cake layers into wedge shapes. Piece the trimmings together on the folded paper, trimming again where necessary, to make a third wedge.

2 Put one wedge on the cake board and spread it thickly with buttercream so that the icing protrudes slightly over the edge. Dot with half the jelly, again adding some near the edges of the cake. Cover with the separate pieces of cake and spread with buttercream and jelly as before, then top with the third wedge.

3 Spread the top and rounded side of the cake with a thin layer of buttercream. Dust your work surface with confectioners' sugar or cornstarch and knead and roll out the white ready-to-use icing to make a triangle, 11 x 10 inches. Drape the icing over the cake, smoothing it into place with your fingertips dusted with a little confectioners' sugar or cornstarch.

4 Trim the icing to the exact shape of the cake. Brush any crumbs off the trimmings, knead again and re-roll. Cut moon shapes, about 4 inches long, to make swags. Curl up the long edges and drape them around the sides, securing them with white decorator frosting.

5 Use a large star tip to pipe rosettes of pink buttercream between the swags and around the top and bottom edges of the cake. Decorate the cake with the sugar flowers. Pipe larger rosettes on top of the cake and press a candle into the center of each.

quick tips

- Cover the cake and board with a plastic cake dome or a large upturned bowl so the cut edges do not dry out. Do not use plastic wrap or foil in case you damage the soft buttercream.

- For a more contemporary look, use different colored icing and replace the flowers with gummy diamonds or other candies.

three naughty kittens

serves 4

decoration time 30 minutes

**8 bought or homemade Cupcakes
(see page 13)**

**single quantity red Buttercream
(see page 15)**

8 oz strawberry-flavored bootlaces

8 inch round silver cake board

**confectioners' sugar or cornstarch,
for dusting**

8 oz black ready-to-use icing

3 oz white ready-to-use icing

6 edible metallic balls

1 tube black decorator frosting

1 If necessary trim the tops of the cakes to level them. Spread a little buttercream over the cake tops and sandwich them together in pairs. Spread buttercream thinly all over the tops and sides of the cakes.

2 Wrap the strawberry bootlaces around the cakes so that the buttercream is completely covered until they resemble balls of yarn. Reserve a few spare strands. Arrange the "balls of yarn" on the cake board and twist the remaining bootlaces between them.

3 Make the kittens. Dust your fingers with confectioners' sugar or cornstarch and use the black icing to mold an oval, 1½ inches long. Put it on top of, or at the base of, a cake and add a small head about ¾ inch in diameter. Shape 4 small legs and a tail and press them on to the body. Make ears with tiny balls of white icing wrapped in black and press them onto the kitten. Press on edible metallic balls for eyes. Add tiny ropes of white for whiskers and stick them on with dots of black decorator frosting. Add tiny balls of white for paws.

4 Repeat to make a second seated black kitten in the same way, but add a circle of white icing to the tummy. Knead the remaining black and white icing together, shape into a tabby cat and arrange on a ball of yarn.

quick tips

- If you like, make an extra kitten so that each child has one to keep or eat.

- If you are short of time, buy little plastic cats from a toy or cake-decorating store.

- A large ball of yarn could be made with 2 cakes made the old-fashioned way in pudding basins.

paint box

serves 6

decoration time 20 minutes

7 inch square bought or homemade Basic Sponge Cake (see page 9) or bought angel cake

8 inch square silver cake board

2 tablespoons smooth apricot jelly

confectioners' sugar or cornstarch, for dusting

8 oz white ready-to-use icing

4 oz red ready-to-use icing

black paste food coloring

5 different colored clear fruit candies or gummy candies

selection of crayon candles

1 Cut the cake in half lengthwise and put both pieces, with the long edges touching, on the cake board at a slight angle. Spread the top and sides of each half with jelly.

2 Dust your work surface with confectioners' sugar or cornstarch and knead and roll out three-quarters of the white icing. Wrap the remaining icing in plastic wrap.

3 Drape the rolled-out icing over the cakes, forming a ridge around the edge and making a cavity for the brush holder and paints. Smooth over the sides and trim off the excess. Knead any trimmings again.

4 Reserve half the red icing to make the paintbrush. Knead and shape the remainder into a rope long enough to go around the base and lid. Flatten it with a rolling pin and cut it into a thin strip with a pastry wheel. Stick it around the edge of the paint box with water.

5 Shape the reserved red icing into a paintbrush handle. Use some of the white trimmings to make the ferrule. Color a little of the remaining white icing black and roll it into a strip. Make a series of cuts almost down to the base, like a fringe, then roll it up for brush bristles. Press the bristles onto the ferrule. Position the brush in the paint box and arrange the candies to resemble paints.

6 Insert the appropriate number of crayon candles into balls of white icing and stick them onto the cake board. Arrange the remaining candles on the lid of the paint box.

quick tips

- For young children use soft gummy candies rather than hard candy.

- Although the cake may be made several days in advance, don't add the candies until just before the party because they will begin to dissolve after a few hours.

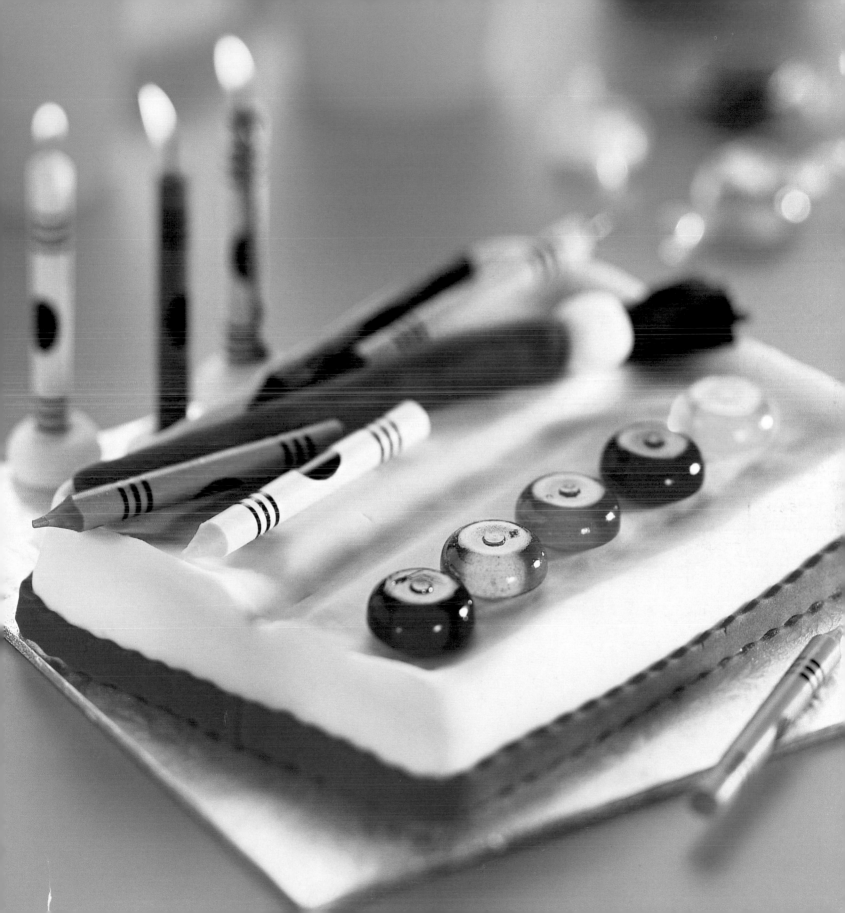

snakes and ladders

serves 12

decoration time 25 minutes

3 bought Battenberg cakes

10 inch square cake board

1 tablespoon smooth apricot jelly

2 lattice-shaped candy bars

confectioners' sugar or cornstarch, for dusting

8 oz white ready-to-use icing

red, yellow, and green paste food colorings

1 tube red decorator frosting

1 tube yellow decorator frosting

edible silver balls

6 different-colored covered chocolate drops

candles and candle-holders

1 Cut the marzipan covering from the cakes and reserve it. Thickly slice the cakes and put the pieces close together on the cake board, arranging them so that the colors alternate to give a checkerboard effect.

2 Cut the reserved marzipan into strips the same thickness as the cake. Brush the edges of the cake with jelly and cover the sides with the marzipan strips.

3 Unwrap the candy bars, cut them into different lengths and arrange the pieces at angles on the cake to make ladders.

4 Dust your work surface with confectioners' sugar or cornstarch. Knead a small piece of white ready-to-use icing, color it red and roll it into a ball. Cut it into a cube to make a die. Cut the remaining icing in half. Color half of it orange with a little red and yellow coloring, and the rest green. Shape a cube of green icing for the second die in the same way as the red one and set aside.

5 Roll some of the remaining green icing into a rope, shape it into a small snake and lift it onto the cake. Make a second, larger orange snake and then an orange and green snake by twisting 2 ropes of colored icing together and curving them into a snake shape. Roll out the green trimmings and use them to make a small arrow. Position the arrow on the bottom left-hand corner to mark the start of the game.

6 Decorate the snakes with zigzag lines of red and yellow decorator frosting. Stick silver balls on the snakes with a little yellow frosting to represent eyes. Arrange the colored candy counters on the cake. Complete with candles to mark the end of the game.

quick tip

- If you can't get lattice-shaped candy bars you could use chocolate sticks for the ladders, with smaller pieces for rungs. Alternatively, you can make the ladders with strips of brown ready-to-use icing.

funny clown

serves 8

decoration time 20 minutes

**7 inch round bought or homemade
Basic Sponge Cake (see page 9)**

**single quantity vanilla Buttercream
(see page 15)**

9 inch round cake board

**confectioners' sugar or cornstarch,
for dusting**

1 lb white ready-to-use icing

4 oz red ready-to-use icing

4 oz blue ready-to-use icing

1 yellow and black licorice candy

**4 oz apple- or strawberry-
flavored bootlaces**

**1 tube green or red
decorator frosting**

1 Sandwich the 2 halves of the cake together with a thick layer of buttercream. Put them on the cake board and spread the top and sides of the cake and the rim of the board thinly with buttercream. Reserve the remaining buttercream.

2 Dust your work surface with confectioners' sugar or cornstarch and knead the white ready-to-use icing. Roll it out until it is large enough to cover the entire cake and rim of the board. Drape the icing over the rolling pin to lift it and smooth it over the cake with your fingertips dusted with confectioners' sugar or cornstarch. Press it over the cake board so that it is firmly in place and trim off the excess.

3 From the red ready-to-use icing shape a ball for the clown's nose and a rope about 5 inches long. Curve the rope and flatten it with a rolling pin for the mouth. Transfer the nose and mouth to the top of the cake, sticking them in place with a little of the remaining buttercream.

4 Knead the blue ready-to-use icing, roll it out thinly and cut out a rectangle, 11 x 2½ inches. Put this on the base of the cake in a wavy line, sticking it in place with dots of buttercream. Re-roll the trimmings and cut 2 eyes and a thin strip for the center of the mouth. Press these onto the cake.

5 Halve the licorice candy and stick it onto the cake for eyeballs. Make the bootlaces curly by wrapping them around the handle of a wooden spoon or metal skewer, hold for 1–2 minutes, then slide off and stick to the cake with decorator frosting for the clown's hair.

quick tips

- If you can't buy ready-colored ready-to-use icing, color your own icing with paste food coloring, but remember that liquid colors do not give the same intensity and too much will make the icing sticky and watery.

- If your children don't like licorice, make the eyeballs with 2 small balls of white icing.

pirate ship

serves 16

decoration time 30 minutes

4 x 10 oz bought double chocolate loaf cakes

14 x 8 inch silver cake board

double quantity chocolate Buttercream (see page 15)

10 oz chocolate finger cookies

8 giant covered chocolate drops

7 long wooden skewers

raffia or fine string

selection of orange, green, and black paper

selection of small plastic pirate figures

shredded blue tissue paper

1 If necessary level the tops of the cakes. Put 2 cakes on the cake board and sandwich the 2 shortest sides together with a little buttercream. Cut one-third off one of the cakes. Spread the top of the cakes with buttercream and stick the other 2 cakes on top with the small slice in the center so that the second layer extends over the first. Cut one end to a point for the prow of the ship and put one of the off-cuts underneath to support it.

2 Spread the remaining buttercream over the top and sides of the cake, then stick chocolate fingers over both sides. Add chocolate drops for portholes.

3 Make the masts. Tie 2 skewers into a cross with a little raffia or string, trimming the sticks if necessary. Repeat to make 2 more. Cut rectangles of paper for sails, make holes along the top edge with a hole punch and lace to the masts with raffia or fine string. Add a hole to the center base of the sails and tie down to the masts. Add a triangular sail to a single stick. Cut a black flag and tape it to the top of one of the masts. Insert the masts into the cake.

4 Complete the cake with plastic pirate figures. Arrange pieces of tissue paper on the cake board to represent the sea.

quick tips

- If you cannot find chocolate loaf cakes the same size as required in the recipe, buy whatever is available and increase or reduce the quantity of icing and the number of finger cookies accordingly. Some loaf cakes have steep domes, so level the tops before using.

- If you prefer, you can cover the cake board with a sea of blue buttercream or shredded coconut, colored blue and held in place with a little jelly.

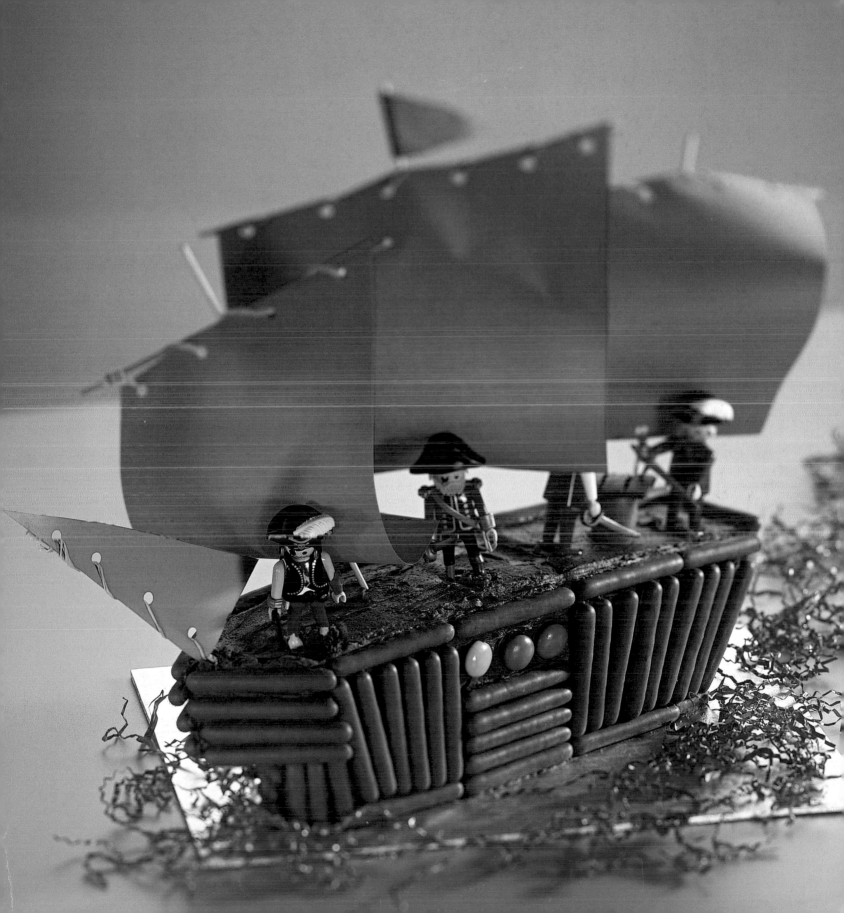

full steam ahead

serves 8

decoration time 30 minutes

2 x 10 oz bought chocolate marble
cakes

11 x 2 inch silver cake board

4 tablespoons smooth apricot jelly

1 lb red ready-to-use icing

confectioners' sugar or cornstarch,
for dusting

6 inch bought plain or chocolate jelly
roll, cut in half

3 oz yellow ready-to-use icing

8 round jelly-filled or iced
ring cookies

1 tube red decorator frosting

2 large red gummy candies

2 large yellow gummy candies

8 oz colored jelly beans

1 candle and candle-holder

1 If necessary trim the tops of the cakes to level them. Put one cake near the end of the cake board. Cut one-third off the remaining cake for the cab and use the remaining piece for the tender. Spread the top and sides of all the cakes with jelly.

2 Reserve one-third of the red icing and wrap it in plastic wrap. Dust your work surface with confectioners' sugar or cornstarch and knead the remaining red icing. Roll out just over half and use it to cover the engine base. Smooth the surface and trim off the excess. Re-roll the trimmings and amalgamate them with the remaining kneaded icing. Use it to cover the cab sides and the jelly roll boiler, leaving the ends of the jelly roll uncovered. Put the cab and boiler in position, securing them with jelly if necessary. If the cab seems a little wobbly, insert a wooden skewer or plastic drinking straw through the cab into the base.

3 Cover the tender in the same way with the reserved red icing, folding the edges of the icing over the top edge of the cake. Put the tender on the cake board behind the engine.

4 Roll out the yellow icing and use it to cover the cab top, to add rectangular windows, and to cover the end of the jelly roll boiler.

5 Stick the cookies to the sides of the engine with red decorator frosting. Add gummy candies to represent buffers and lights, sticking them in place with red decorator frosting. Pipe a number on front of the boiler. Fill the tender with jelly beans and complete the engine with a candle and candle-holder.

quick tips

- If you are having lots of children to a party add extra trucks of candies, made in the same way as the tender, and arrange the cake on a long strip of cardboard or a thin piece of wood covered with foil or paper. You could add a chocolate finger cookie track with sugar crystals or Demerara sugar for gravel.

- The tender could be filled with covered chocolate drops or chocolate buttons instead of jelly beans.

twelfth night crown

serves 8

decoration time 20 minutes

7 inch round bought or homemade
Basic Sponge Cake (see page 9)

single quantity orange-flavored
Buttercream (see page 15)

9 inch round cake board

4 tablespoons sugar balls

confectioners' sugar or cornstarch,
for dusting

1 lb yellow
ready-to-use icing

16 black jelly beans

9 clear fruit candies

1 tube yellow decorator frosting

1 Cut the cake in half horizontally and sandwich the layers together with some of the buttercream. Put them on the cake board and spread buttercream thinly over the sides of the cake and thickly over the top. Sprinkle sugar balls over the top.

2 Dust your work surface with confectioners' sugar or cornstarch. Knead and roll out the yellow ready-to-use icing and trim it to a rectangle, 24 x 3½ inches. Use a plain 2½ inch cookie cutter to scallop the top edge, then carefully press the strip of icing around the edge of the cake.

3 Knead the trimmings and shape them into a rope, 24 inches long. Press the rope to the base of the cake, trimming the ends if necessary and sticking it in place with a little buttercream. Spread the remaining buttercream over the icing rope to resemble a fur trim. Decorate with black jelly beans.

4 Stick the clear fruit candies onto the crown for jewels, using a generous quantity of decorator frosting to hold them in place.

quick tips

- You could cover the top of the cake with rumpled red or blue ready-to-use icing to give the impression of velvet.

- Don't add the clear fruit candies until the last moment because they might dissolve if left to stand for any length of time. You need to be quite generous with the decorator frosting or you will find that the candies start to slide off the crown.

penguins' igloo

serves 8

decoration time 30 minutes

3 tablespoons smooth apricot jelly

6 inch round bought or homemade
filled Basic Sponge Cakes
(see page 9)

11 inch round cake board, plain or
iced

confectioners' sugar or cornstarch,
for dusting

1 lb white ready-to-use icing

1 bought mini-jelly roll

4 tablespoons shredded coconut

8 oz black ready-to-use icing

1 oz red ready-to-use icing

14 edible silver balls

1 Spread a little jelly over the top of one of the cakes and put the second cake on top. Use a small serrated knife to cut away the edges of the top cake to make a domed igloo shape. Spread the top and sides of the cakes with jelly and put it on the cake board just off center.

2 Dust your work surface with confectioners' sugar or cornstarch. Knead the white ready-to-use icing and roll it out to a circle 10 inches across. Drape the icing over the cake and smooth it over the top and sides. Trim off the excess and knead the trimmings.

3 Cut the mini-jelly roll in half and put one piece on top of the other, sticking it in place with jelly. Roll out a little of the remaining white ready-to-use icing and use it to cover the mini-jelly roll, pressing a door shape in one end. Butt the mini-roll up against the igloo, sticking it in place with jelly. Use a small knife to mark snow bricks all over the igloo and tunnel entrance.

4 Shape the remaining white icing into small balls and set them aside. Sprinkle coconut around the base of the igloo.

5 Make the penguins. Shape black ready-to-use icing into 5 small balls and the same number of slightly larger balls. Press the small balls on top of the larger ones to make the penguins' heads and bodies. Roll the remaining black icing into 5 ropes, each about 2 inches long. Flatten the ropes with your fingertips, shaping the ends into points, and wrap them around the penguin bodies for wings. Add tiny triangles of red icing for beaks and silver balls for eyes.

6 Press 5 of the smaller white balls of icing into ovals and press them onto the penguins' tummies. Arrange the penguins on the cake and add the remaining small balls of white icing for snowballs.

quick tips

- If you make your own cakes you will need to make 2 pairs and fill them with buttercream or jelly.

- Cover the cake board with 8 oz blue ready-to-use icing and stick it onto the cake board with a little smooth apricot jelly, spread around the outer edges of the board.

the doyouthinkhesawus dinosaur

serves 10

decoration time 30 minutes

9 inch round bought or homemade Basic Sponge Cake (see page 9)

6 tablespoons smooth apricot jelly

10 x 14 inch rectangular or 15 inch oval cake board

1 lb white ready-to-use icing

green, blue, and yellow paste food colorings

confectioners' sugar or cornstarch, for dusting

8 oz red ready-to-use icing

2 oz package covered chocolate drops

1 tube yellow decorator frosting

sugar crystals

1 Cut a 1½ inch strip from the center of the cake, then sandwich together the half-moon shapes with some of the jelly. Stand the cake on the board so that the curved sides are uppermost. Halve the remaining strip of cake and use one half for the head, rounding off the corners to make the snout and back of the head. Use the other half for the tail, cutting a diagonal slice off the length of the tail piece. Turn it around and butt the pieces together to lengthen the tail. Brush the top and sides of the cake with apricot jelly.

2 Knead the white icing to soften it, then mix in a little green coloring until it is evenly colored. Add more green, blue, and yellow colorings and knead briefly for a marbled effect. Dust your work surface with confectioners' sugar or cornstarch and roll out the icing until it is large enough to cover the dinosaur. Drape the icing over the cake, smooth the surface, and trim off the excess. Cut a triangle for the end of the tail, shape legs, eyes, and nostrils from the trimmings and stick them onto the cake with the remaining jelly.

3 Knead the red icing. Shape small balls of the icing into triangles and press them along the top of the dinosaur for back spines. Roll out and cut a tongue and press it on the mouth.

4 Stick the candies on the dinosaur's back and eye sockets with yellow decorator frosting, then pipe on eyeballs. Sprinkle sugar crystals on the board around the dinosaur.

quick tips

- The cake could be flavored with a little grated orange zest and sandwiched together with one quantity of plain or orange-flavored Buttercream (see page 15).

- Recycle old cake boards and cover marks or scratches with new foil or colored ready-to-use icing, sticking it in place with a little jelly, or shredded coconut.

three little pigs

serves 12

decoration time 30 minutes

1 bought triple variety pack or
3 square homemade flavored Basic
Sponge Cakes (see page 9),
each 9 oz

12 x 10 inch rectangular cake board

12 oz bought chocolate-chip cake
or other flavored loaf cake with
sloping sides

double quantity plain Buttercream
(see page 15)

1 tablespoon cocoa powder dissolved
in 1 tablespoon boiling water

green paste food coloring

confectioners' sugar, for dusting

2 oz each blue, red, and green
ready-to-use icing

8 oz yellow ready-to-use icing

5 oz package chocolate sticks

8 oz luxury milk chocolate

2½ oz chocolate fingers

4 oz pink ready-to-use icing

2 oz gray ready-to-use icing

1 multipack of colored decorator
frosting to include black, red, yellow,
and green

⅔ cup shredded coconut

1 Put the cakes on the board. Cut the loaf cake into 3 and use buttercream to stick one piece on top of each of the other cakes for the roofs. Spoon one-third of the remaining buttercream into a bowl and flavor the remainder with cocoa paste. Spread plain buttercream all over one house, then color any remaining icing green. Spread all the chocolate buttercream over the other houses.

2 Dust your work surface with confectioners' sugar and roll out the blue icing. Cut out a door shape for the first house. Roll out the green and red icing and add doors and doorknobs to the other houses.

3 Make the house of straw. Knead and roll out the yellow icing. Cut it into 4 squares, each 2 x 2 inches, mark lines with a knife to look like straw, then press them onto the cake.

4 Make the house of sticks. Cover the house with the green door with chocolate sticks, sticking some on the roof at angles.

5 Make the house of bricks. Cut the milk chocolate into pieces and stick them over the front and sides of the last cake, adding a double square for the chimney. Add finger cookies for the roof.

6 Shape the pigs. For each pig use 3 balls of pink ready-to-use icing, a large ball for the body, a medium-size ball for the head, and a small ball for the nose. Add tiny balls, shaped into points, for ears and larger balls for feet, each with 3 small cuts. Roll tiny ropes and twist them into tails.

7 Make a wolf in the same way with the gray icing, but shape the circular head into more of a snout and mark the sides of the head to look like whiskers. Position the pigs and wolf on and by the houses, sticking any parts together with water. Mark nostrils with a knife and pipe on black eyes.

8 Spread green buttercream thinly over the cake board, color the coconut green and scatter it over the board. Complete the houses with numbers piped onto the doors.

quick tip

- If you're short of time, leave the cake board undecorated and simply arrange the cakes on a green foil tray.

soccer boots

serves 14

decoration time 30 minutes

2 x 8 inch bought or homemade
Jelly Rolls (see page 12)

2 tablespoons smooth apricot jelly

confectioners' sugar or cornstarch,
for dusting

1 lb black ready-to-use icing

4 oz gray ready-to-use icing

4 oz white ready-to-use icing

3 flat licorice bootlaces

large tissue-lined shoe box

about 10 foil-wrapped
chocolate soccerballs

1 Use a small, sharp knife to round off 2 ends of each of the jelly rolls to make the heels. Out of the top of each cake scoop an oval, about 4 x 2 inches and ¾ inch deep in the center. Make a sloping cut from the front of the scooped-out area down to the front end of each cake. Round off all the edges. Brush the jelly over the cakes.

2 Dust your work surface with confectioners' sugar or cornstarch and roll out half the black icing to a rectangle, 12 x 8 inches. Lay the icing over one cake, pressing it down into the cavity. Ease the icing to fit around the sides and tuck the ends under the boot. Dust the palms of your hands with confectioners' sugar or cornstarch and smooth the icing. Cover the other cake with the remaining black icing in the same way.

3 Roll out half the gray icing into 2 ovals, each 4½ x 2½ inches, and press them into the cavities in the tops of the boots. Halve the reserved gray icing and shape 2 boot tongues, each about 5 inches long and 2½ inches across the top. Use a dampened paintbrush to secure them in position. (If the ends of the flaps flop into the cavity, prop them up with some crumpled paper towels until the icing has hardened.)

4 Roll out the white icing and cut it into long strips about ¾ inch wide. Arrange them on the boots, rounding off the corners at the front and tucking the ends around the back.

5 Cut the licorice into 14 pieces, each about 1½ inches long, and use them for the laces, making holes in the white icing so that you can easily press in the ends. Use longer lengths of licorice for the trailing ends.

6 Line a shoe box with tissue paper and arrange the boots in the box. Scatter the foil-wrapped balls around the cakes.

quick tip

- For quick soccer boots shape 2 jelly rolls as described for the Ballet Shoes (see page 26) but cover them with black ready-to-use icing with a paler gray liner. Add studs made with balls of black icing, colored flashes made with strips of green or red ready-to-use icing, and laces of licorice or black icing.

box of toys

serves 24

decoration time 30 minutes

7 inch square bought or homemade
Rich Fruit Cake, covered with almond
paste (see pages 11 and 21 for
recipe and technique)

10 inch square plate or cake board

confectioners' sugar or cornstarch,
for dusting

1 lb white ready-to-use icing

8 oz dark green ready-to-use icing

1 oz red ready-to-use icing

selection of small wooden or plastic
toys for decoration

1 tube green or red
decorator frosting

36 inches fine red ribbon

1 Put the cake on the plate or board. Dust your work surface with confectioners' sugar or cornstarch and roll out the white icing to a 12 inch square. Lay it over the cake, smoothing the icing around the sides and trimming off the excess around the base.

2 Thinly roll out the green icing to a 9 inch square. Use a sharp knife to trim the edges into deep scallops.

3 Lightly brush the top of the cake with a dampened paintbrush and lay the green icing over the cake so that the scalloped edges fall around the sides.

4 Roll the red icing into small balls and secure one to the tip of each scallop. Arrange the small toys on top of the cake, securing them with dots of decorator frosting. Tie the ribbon around the cake's base.

quick tip

• The best place to buy little toys for decorating this cake is a toy store with a good selection of tiny "stocking fillers." Add to these a few small cake decorations—Santas and snowmen—and you'll quickly accumulate a colorful collection. Remove them all from the cake before cutting.

animal ark

serves 28

decoration time about 1½ hours

3 x 12 oz packs of fun-size flaked chocolate bars

5 inch and 7 inch square bought or homemade Rich Chocolate Cakes (see page 10)

triple quantity chocolate Buttercream (see page 15)

10 inch square plate

8 oz pink ready-to-use icing

8 oz chocolate brown ready-to-use icing

8 oz light brown ready-to-use icing

8 oz yellow ready-to-use icing

black food coloring

1 Trim the flaked chocolate bars so that they are ½ inch longer than the cakes. Cut each cake into 3 layers and then sandwich with buttercream. Put the larger cake on the plate and spread it with more buttercream. Position the smaller cake on top and spread it with the remaining buttercream.

2 Using a fine-bladed knife, carefully cut each chocolate bar in half. Position the pieces around the sides of the cakes.

3 Make the elephants. For each roll out a small ball of pink icing into an oval. Press it into the buttercream. Take a larger ball of icing and mold a flattened pear shape, gradually elongating the thin end into a trunk. Cut off the tip of the trunk and impress lines along it with a knife. Prop the icing against the pink base, securing it with a dampened paintbrush. Shape and secure large floppy ears.

4 Make the monkeys. For each roll a small ball of chocolate brown icing for the head and press it into the buttercream. Shape large round ears and secure them to the sides of the head. Secure a flattened ball of light brown icing for the snout.

5 Make the lions. For each roll out a small ball of yellow icing into an oval and press it into the buttercream. Flatten a piece of brown icing for the mane and indent it around the edges with your fingertips. Roll another ball of icing and flatten it against the mane. Position it on the yellow base. Add ears and a thin rope of icing for the tail.

6 Make the bears. For each roll out a small ball of light brown icing into an oval and press it into the buttercream. Roll a larger ball of icing and position it for the head, adding 2 small, round ears. Secure a flattened ball of icing for the snout. Make paws from the icing trimmings. Use a fine paintbrush and black food coloring to add features to the animals' faces.

quick tips

• Rich and chocolaty, this cake would make a great "alternative" christening cake.

• The animals are a bit fiddly, but you can make them several weeks in advance and store them in an airtight container, so that you can complete the cake a couple of days in advance.

princess cakes

makes 12

decoration time 20 minutes

single quantity Buttercream
(see page 15)

pink food coloring

12 bought or homemade Cupcakes
(see page 13)

edible silver balls

1 Divide the buttercream in half and add a few drops of pink food coloring to one bowl. Mix well to color the buttercream. Use a small spatula to spread the pink buttercream over the tops of the cakes to within ¼ inch of the edges, doming it up slightly in the center.

2 Put half the white buttercream in a pastry bag fitted with a writing tip and the remainder in a bag fitted with a star tip. Pipe lines, ½ inch apart, across the pink buttercream, and then across in the other direction to make a diamond pattern.

3 Use the icing in the other bag to pipe little stars around the edges. Decorate the piped lines with silver balls.

quick tip

• If you can find them, use silver-colored paper bake cups to make these little cakes even more suitable for a princess.

flower garden

makes 12

decoration time 30 minutes

12 bought or homemade Cupcakes
(see page 13)

single quantity green Buttercream
(see page 15)

confectioners' sugar or cornstarch,
for dusting

12 oz white ready-to-use icing

1 tube pink gel decorator frosting

1 If necessary, trim the tops of the cakes to level them, then spread them with green buttercream.

2 Dust your work surface with confectioners' sugar or cornstarch and knead and roll out the white icing. Stamp out flower shapes using 1 inch and ½ inch cutters. Curve the flowers by pressing them into a clean, dry sponge or the cupped palm of your hand with the handle of a wooden spoon. Alternatively, if you have them, use plunger cutters.

3 Arrange the flowers randomly over the cakes. Finish each flower with a dot of pink gel frosting. Arrange on a plate or cake board to serve.

quick tips

• You can buy tiny cutters, often described as aspic cutters, in good cookstores or specialty cake-decorating stores, where they may be available with easy-to-press-out plungers.

• If you have lots of food to prepare for a party, cook the cakes in advance and pack them into a plastic bag or box when they are cold. Prepare the buttercream in advance and put it in a small plastic box. Freeze both until the day before the party. Decorate the cakes the night before or on the morning of the party.

funny faces

makes 12

decoration time 20 minutes

3 oz luxury dark cooking chocolate, broken into pieces

12 bought or homemade Cupcakes (see page 13)

single quantity Buttercream (see page 15)

pink or brown paste food coloring

selection of small covered chocolate drops

1 tube red decorator frosting

sugar flowers (optional)

1 Set a heatproof bowl over a small saucepan of water. Bring the water to a boil, then remove from the heat. Add the chocolate to the bowl and leave for 2–3 minutes until melted.

2 If the cakes have high domes, trim them slightly to level them. Color the buttercream to a skin tone, then spread it over the tops of the cakes.

3 Add candies for eyes and pipe on red mouths. Stir the chocolate and spoon it into a waxed paper pastry bag. Snip off the tip and pipe on hair, glasses, and eye details. Add sugar flowers to the girls' hair styles if you like, then leave the cakes in a cool place until the chocolate has set.

quick tips

- You can use colored tubes of decorator frosting for hair instead of the melted chocolate.

- Use the ideas here as a starting point to add a more personal touch and decorate the cakes to look like the members of your family or your child's friends. If you have time, shape ready-to-use icing hats, scarves, bowties, or even arms and legs.

- Make these cakes multiracial by coloring the buttercream with pink food coloring, melted chocolate, or brown food coloring.

dominoes

makes 18

decoration time 20 minutes

12 x 9 x 2 inch plain or orange-flavored Basic Sponge Cake (see page 9)

double quantity vanilla- or orange-flavored Buttercream (see page 15)

2 tubes covered chocolate drops

2 oz strawberry-flavored bootlaces

1 With the longest edge of the cake nearest you, cut it into 3 bars, each 3 inches wide. Cut each piece into 6 small bars.

2 Spread buttercream over the top of the cakes and then decorate with groups of colored candies to resemble domino dots. Separate the 2 sets of dots with a strip of bootlace and then press lengths of bootlace around the edges of the cakes to make borders. Arrange on a plate or cake board and serve.

quick tips

• Plain uncut cake can be frozen and then decorated with buttercream and frozen without the candies. Alternatively, use bought cake bars. These are ideal if you have only a couple of children for tea because they are so quick to defrost.

• You could also make the cakes into little sums by stamping out numbers, crosses for addition and multiplication, single strips for subtraction, and double strips for the equals signs.

ladybugs

makes 12

decoration time 30 minutes

2 tablespoons raspberry or strawberry jelly

12 bought or homemade Cupcakes (see page 13)

confectioners' sugar or cornstarch, for dusting

6 oz red ready-to-use icing

4 oz black ready-to-use icing

½ oz white ready-to-use icing

small piece of candied orange rind, cut into matchstick lengths

1 Use a pastry brush to cover the top of each cake with jelly. Dust your work surface with confectioners' sugar or cornstarch and knead the red ready-to-use icing. Roll it out thinly and cut 12 circles with a plain 2½ inch cookie cutter. Put a red circle on top of each cake.

2 Roll out thin strips of black ready-to-use icing and position one across each red circle, securing with a dampened paintbrush. Roll out half the remaining black icing to a thin sausage shape, about ½ inch in diameter. Cut the black icing into thin slices and secure to the cakes to represent ladybug spots.

3 From the remaining black icing shape oval heads and secure them in position. Roll small balls of the white ready-to-use icing for eyes and press tiny balls of black icing over them. Secure with a dampened paintbrush.

4 Make the ladybugs' antennae. Press the lengths of candied orange rind into position behind the heads, pressing small balls of black icing on the ends. Use tiny pieces of white icing to shape smiling mouths.

quick tip

• If you cannot find candied orange rind, which is cut into strips and used for the antennae, use small chocolate sticks instead.

building blocks

makes 9

decoration time 30 minutes

8 inch square homemade plain or
flavored Basic Sponge Cake
(see page 9)

double quantity Buttercream
(see page 15)

1 lb red ready-to-use icing

confectioners' sugar or cornstarch,
for dusting

1 lb blue ready-to-use icing

1 lb yellow ready-to-use icing

2 tubes covered chocolate drops

1 tube yellow decorator frosting

1 tube red decorator frosting

candles and candle-holders (optional)

1 If necessary, level the surface of the cake and then cut it into 9 even-size blocks.

2 Spread the tops and sides of the cake blocks thinly with buttercream, leaving the bases plain.

3 Lightly knead the red icing, then roll it out thinly on a surface lightly dusted with confectioners' sugar or cornstarch to a 15 x 8 inch rectangle. Cut it into 15 squares, then stick them onto the cakes. Repeat with the blue, then the yellow icing, until all the butter-iced sides of the cakes are covered.

4 Stick candies around the edges of the cakes with decorator frosting, then pipe letters or numbers. Stack the cakes on a cake board, adding candles to the tops of some of the cakes, if desired.

quick tips

- Larger packages of ready-colored ready-to-use icing can be bought from specialty cake-decorating stores. If you don't have one near you, color plain white icing with paste food colorings instead.

- For very little children, the blocks could be cut smaller, making 16 instead, but do allow extra time as they will be more fiddly to ice.

counting cakes

makes 12

decoration time 15 minutes

single quantity Buttercream (see page 15)

green or yellow food coloring

12 bought or homemade Cupcakes (see page 13)

confectioners' sugar or cornstarch, for dusting

6 oz white ready-to-use icing

2 oz red ready-to-use icing

2 oz blue ready-to-use icing

colored sugar sprinkles

1 Color the buttercream with green or yellow food coloring and use a small spatula to spread it all over the tops of the cakes.

2 Dust your work surface with confectioners' sugar or cornstarch. Knead the white ready-to-use icing, roll it out and use a plain 2½ inch round cookie cutter to cut out 12 circles. Gently press one on the top of each cake.

3 Roll out the red ready-to-use icing and cut out half the numbers. Secure to the cakes with a dampened paintbrush. Use the blue ready-to-use icing for the remaining numbers.

4 Lightly brush the edges of the white icing with a dampened paintbrush and scatter over the sugar sprinkles.

quick tip

- Cut out the numbers by hand using a sharp knife or use small number cookie cutters. The numbers could simply run from 1 to 12, or you could represent the ages of the party-goers, if appropriate.

chocolate hedgehogs

makes 6

decoration time 20 minutes

6 bought or homemade Cupcakes (see page 13)

single quantity dark Chocolate Fudge Frosting (see page 18)

3 flaked chocolate bars, cut into thin pieces

3 candied cherries, halved

12 edible silver balls or small covered chocolate drops

1 Remove the cakes from the paper cups and cut a triangular snout in each cake. Put them on a wire rack set over a large plate.

2 Spoon warm chocolate frosting over the cakes until they are completely covered. Working quickly, stick pieces of flaked chocolate over two-thirds of each cake to represent the spines. Add cherry noses and silver-ball or chocolate-drop eyes.

3 Carefully lift the hedgehogs onto a cake board or plate, trimming away any surplus icing around the base.

quick tips

- If children are helping you make the cakes, it might be easier to frost and decorate them one at a time, because the frosting sets quickly, making it more difficult to press the chocolate spines onto the cakes.

- Nestle the hedgehogs on a grassy board by coloring a little shredded coconut with liquid green food coloring and spooning it around the finished cakes.

space bugs

makes 12

decoration time 25 minutes

12 chocolate or plain, bought or
homemade Cupcakes (see page 13)

4 tablespoons chocolate spread

confectioners' sugar or cornstarch,
for dusting

12 oz red ready-to-use icing

12 chocolate-covered marshmallows

12 chocolate sticks

1 tube red decorator frosting

1 package small covered
chocolate drops

1 tube black decorator frosting

1 Leave the cakes in their paper cups and, if necessary, trim the tops to level them. Spread the cakes with chocolate spread.

2 Dust your work surface with confectioners' sugar or cornstarch. Knead the red ready-to-use icing, roll it out and cut 12 rounds with a plain 2¼ inch cookie cutter. Cut a little off the top of each round using the same cutter, then cut the remaining shapes in half to make wings. Press the wings onto the cakes so that the tips are slightly apart. Re-roll the trimmings as needed and continue until all the cakes are covered.

3 Add the marshmallows for heads, sticking them in place with a little extra chocolate spread if necessary. Halve the chocolate sticks and press 2 behind each head for antennae. Pipe on red smiling mouths, pipe dots of red icing over the wings and stick on the candies. Add chocolate-drop eyes to the faces and the tops of the antennae in the same way. Pipe black icing dots on the eyes. Arrange the bugs on a cake board or plate. Leave in a cool place to harden.

quick tips

- If you don't have a cookie cutter the right size, use an upturned glass as a template.

- Look out for ready-colored icing from specialty cake-decorating stores. Supermarkets do sell colored icing, but it is usually in a box containing 3 or 4 small packs of different colors and can be expensive if you only need one. Alternatively, buy white icing and color it yourself with red paste coloring.

- For Halloween make up beetles with brown or black ready-to-use icing. Omit the spots or pipe on squiggly markings with tubes of colored decorator frosting.

on the farm

makes 12

decoration time 45 minutes

½ **quantity Buttercream
(see page 15)**

**12 bought or homemade Cupcakes
(see pages 13)**

4 oz brown ready-to-use icing

**confectioners' sugar or cornstarch,
for dusting**

4 oz yellow ready-to-use icing

4 oz pink ready-to-use icing

½ **oz white ready-to-use icing**

½ **oz black ready-to-use icing**

black food coloring

1 Use a spatula to spread a thick layer of the buttercream over 4 of the cakes and lightly peak (these will become the sheep). Spread the rest of the buttercream over the remaining cakes.

2 Make the sheep. Take 3 oz of the brown ready-to-use icing, wrapping the remainder in plastic wrap. Dust your work surface with confectioners' sugar or cornstarch and knead the icing. Reserve a small piece for the ears and roll the remainder into 4 balls. Flatten each ball into an oval shape and gently press on the cakes thickly spread with buttercream. Shape and position small ears on each sheep.

3 Make the cows. Reserve a small piece of the yellow ready-to-use icing for the ears. Roll the remainder into 4 balls and flatten into ovals as large as the cake tops. Gently press onto 4 more cakes. Shape and position the ears. Use the remaining brown ready-to-use icing to shape the cows' nostrils and horns, securing with a dampened paintbrush.

4 Make the pigs. Reserve 1 oz of the pink ready-to-use icing for the snouts and ears. Roll the remainder into 4 balls and flatten them into rounds, almost as large as each cake top. Shape and position the snouts and floppy ears, pressing 2 small holes in each snout with the tip of a toothpick or fine skewer.

5 Use the white and black icing to make all the animals' eyes, changing the shape and size to suit each animal. Roll small balls of white icing and press tiny balls of black icing over them. Secure with a dampened paintbrush. Use a fine paintbrush, dipped in the black food coloring, to paint on additional features.

quick tip

- Lightly dusting your work surface with confectioners' sugar or cornstarch will help stop the icing sticking to the surface and will smooth and polish the icing when it's on the cake. Cornstarch is better if you're working with dark reds and blues because it disappears as you smooth, while confectioners' sugar may leave a faint white mark.

snakes in the jungle

makes 12

decoration time 45 minutes

2 tablespoons strawberry or raspberry jelly

12 bought or homemade Cupcakes (see page 13)

confectioners' sugar or cornstarch, for dusting

6 oz green ready-to-use icing

4 flaked chocolate bars, cut into 2 inch lengths

2 oz red ready-to-use icing

2 oz yellow ready-to-use icing

2 oz white ready-to-use icing

1 oz black ready-to-use icing

1 Use a pastry brush to cover the top of each cake with jelly. Dust your work surface with confectioners' sugar or cornstarch and knead the green ready-to-use icing. Roll it out thinly and cut 12 circles with a plain 2½ inch cookie cutter. Put a green circle on top of each cake.

2 Make a snake. Take about ¼ oz of ready-to-use icing and roll it under the palm of your hand to form a thin sausage about 5–6 inches long, tapering it to a point at one end and shaping a head at the other. Flatten the head slightly and mark a mouth with a small, sharp knife.

3 Thinly roll out a little ready-to-use icing in a contrasting color and cut out small diamond shapes. Secure along the snake using a dampened paintbrush. Wrap the snake around a length of flaked chocolate and position on top of a cake.

4 Make more snakes in the same way, kneading together small amounts of the colored ready-to-use icing to make different colors. For some of the cakes, press the chocolate bar vertically into the cake.

5 To make the snakes' eyes roll small balls of white icing and press tiny balls of black icing over them. Secure to the snakes' heads with a dampened paintbrush.

quick tip

• **As long as you have green icing for the cake bases you can make the snakes in any colors you like. Orange can easily be made by blending red and yellow icing, and pink by blending red and white.**

2
birthday cakes

big birthday

serves 45–50

decoration time 1 hour

6 inch, 8 inch, and 10 inch round
bought or homemade Basic Sponge
Cakes (see page 9) or Rich Chocolate
Cakes (see page 10)

12 inch plate

quadruple quantity Buttercream (see
page 15) or triple quantity White
Chocolate Ganache (see page 17)

confectioners' sugar or cornstarch,
for dusting

8 oz dark red ready-to-use icing

8 oz dark blue ready-to-use icing

8 oz purple ready-to-use icing

1 tube red or blue decorator frosting

number birthday candles
(e.g., 18 or 21)

fine blue and purple parcel ribbon

1 Put the largest cake on the plate and spread it with a scant half of the buttercream or ganache, smoothing it with a spatula.

2 Put the medium-size cake on top and spread it with more buttercream or ganache in the same way. Position the smallest cake on top and spread it evenly with the remaining buttercream or ganache.

3 Dust your work surface with confectioners' sugar or cornstarch and shape the colored icings into little parcel shapes. Use the decorator frosting to pipe ribbons on the parcels.

4 Position the candles on top of the cake, then drape lengths of ribbon over the top and down the sides of the cake. Tuck the parcels in among the ribbons.

quick tips

- Celebratory candles are available in all numbers, so this is a quick and easy celebration cake for any important birthday.

- Cover the cake with buttercream or ganache a day in advance and keep it in a cool place.

- The cake can also be decorated with ready-to-use icing. You will need about 4 lb. Cover each cake separately with icing before stacking them on the plate.

50th birthday

serves 30

preparation time 10 minutes, plus cooling

cooking time about 50 minutes

decoration time 1 hour

large 5 and 0 number cake pans

2 x 5-egg quantity Basic Sponge Cake mixture (see page 9)

double quantity Buttercream (see page 15)

8 tablespoons smooth raspberry or strawberry jelly

confectioners' sugar or cornstarch, for dusting

1½ lb pale blue ready-to-use icing

18 x 14 inch rectangular cake board

10 oz chocolate brown ready-to-use icing

2 lb dark blue ready-to-use icing

8–10 tea lights

6 feet brown ribbon for edges of cake board

1 Grease and line the number pans and put them on a large cookie sheet. Divide the cake mixture between the pans and level the surface. Bake in a preheated oven, 325°F, for about 50 minutes or until just firm and a tester, inserted into the centers, comes out clean. Allow to cool.

2 Cut the cakes in half horizontally and sandwich the layers with the buttercream and half the jelly. Spread the remaining jelly over the tops and sides of the cakes.

3 Dust your work surface with confectioners' sugar or cornstarch and roll out 1 lb of the pale blue icing to a rectangle that is slightly smaller than the cake board. Dampen the board and lift the icing onto the board. Smooth it down gently with the palms of your hands and trim the icing, leaving a border ¾ inch wide around the edges of the board.

4 Thinly roll out 8 oz of the brown icing and cut out long strips. Use these to cover the edges of the board, trimming off the excess around the edges. Reserve the trimmings.

5 Roll out half the dark blue icing and use it to cover one of the numbers, easing the icing down the sides and trimming off the excess around the base. If necessary patch up any gaps around the sides. Carefully transfer the cake to the board. Cover the second cake with the remaining icing and put it on the board.

6 Roll the remaining pale blue and brown icing into long, thin ropes. Twist them together and cut into manageable lengths. Drape over the cakes, securing with a dampened paintbrush. Arrange the tea lights around the numbers and secure the brown ribbon around the sides of the board.

quick tips

- This is a great cake for a large party of adults. It cuts into plenty of portions, is not too difficult to ice and works well for any age. Large number pans can be hired for a couple of days for making the cake.

- It's easier to ice the centers of numbers such as 0, 6, 8, and 9 with a strip of icing before you cover the rest of the cake.

birthday present

serves 40

decoration time 30 minutes

9 inch square bought or homemade Rich Fruit Cake, covered with almond paste (see pages 11 and 21 for recipe and technique)

12 inch square cake board

3 lb white ready-to-use icing

dark red or pink food coloring

confectioners' sugar or cornstarch, for dusting

6 feet soft gray ribbon, about 1 inch wide

6 feet pale pink ribbon, about 2 inches wide

pale pink ribbon for edges of cake board

1 Put the cake on the board. Reserve 8 oz of the icing and lightly knead the remainder. Use a toothpick to dot the icing carefully and cautiously with food coloring. The more color you add, the more vibrant the finished result will be.

2 Roll out the icing to a thick sausage. Fold it into 3 and roll again, repeating the process until the icing is marbled with color. Dust your work surface with confectioners' sugar or cornstarch and roll out the icing to a square that will cover the cake. Smooth the icing down the sides and trim off the excess around the base.

3 Lay the narrower ribbon over the wider ribbon. Use the tip of a knife to tuck the ends of the ribbons under the base of the cake on one side. Bring the ribbons over to the other side and cut to fit, tucking the ends under the cake. Repeat on the other 2 sides and shape a generous bow for the top. Secure the bow in position with clear adhesive tape.

4 Use the reserved white icing to cover the edges of the cake board. Secure the pink ribbon around the edges of the board.

quick tips

- The ribbons are the focal point of this easy cake, so choose soft, delicate colors for a romantic look, or use an alternative color scheme for a bolder effect.

- Instead of fruit cake, you could use a bought or homemade sponge cake, sandwiched with buttercream.

man's best friend

serves 24

decoration time about 1 hour

10 inch round bought or homemade Basic Sponge Cake (see page 9) or Rich Chocolate Cake (see page 10)

triple quantity Chocolate Fudge Frosting (see page 18)

12 inch round plate

14 oz light brown ready-to-use icing

confectioners' sugar or cornstarch, for dusting

8 oz blue ready-to-use icing

dark blue or black food coloring

1 Halve the cake horizontally and sandwich the layers together with one-third of the chocolate fudge frosting. Put it on the plate and use a spatula to swirl the remainder of the fudge frosting over the top and sides of the cake.

2 Make the dog. Roll an 8 oz ball of brown icing for the body and flatten it slightly. Put it on the center of the cake. Roll a 6 oz ball of icing for the head. Pinch one side to a point to make a muzzle. Rest the head, tilting it slightly to one side, at one end of the body. From the remaining icing shape small paws, droopy ears, and a curved tail. Position the paws and ears and reserve the tail.

3 Dust your work surface with confectioners' sugar or cornstarch and thinly roll out the blue icing. Cut out an 8 inch square. Drape the icing over the cake, fitting it first around the dog's head and draping it across the cake in loose folds. Position the tail.

4 Use a fine paintbrush and the blue or black food coloring to paint closed eyes, a nose, and a mouth on the dog's face.

quick tip

• It's not only children who like animal cakes— there are plenty of adults who would find this cake appealing. The dog can easily be made to resemble the recipient's own dog by changing the color of the icing and by painting on spots or patches as appropriate.

triple chocolate croquembouche

serves 10–12

preparation time 20 minutes

cooking time 20 minutes

decoration time 30 minutes

40 Choux Pastry Buns (see page 14)

double quantity White Chocolate Ganache (see page 17)

8 oz dark chocolate

flat plate, at least 11 inches across

8 oz milk chocolate

12–15 gold-colored chocolate dragées, roughly chopped

1 When the choux pastry buns are cool, fill each one with a heaping teaspoon of the white chocolate ganache.

2 Break half the dark chocolate into pieces and put them in a bowl over a saucepan of lightly simmering water until the chocolate has melted. Dip the base of about 10 buns in the melted chocolate and arrange them in a circle, about 9 inches across, on the serving plate. (When it sets, the chocolate will hold the buns together.) Put about 3 buns in the center.

3 Gradually build up layers of buns to form a cone shape, dipping each bun in melted chocolate so that it is secured to the buns underneath. Finish with a single bun on top.

4 Melt the remaining dark chocolate and the milk chocolate in separate bowls and spoon over the buns. Tuck the chocolate dragées in among the buns to finish. Keep the cake in a cool place until ready to serve.

quick tips

• Make the buns in advance, put them in plastic bags and freeze them, crisping them in a moderate oven for 5 minutes before use.

• If you're assembling the croquembouche in hot weather you might need to chill it halfway through so that it doesn't collapse.

white chocolate frosted cake

serves 12

decoration time 20 minutes

7 inch round bought or homemade Basic Sponge Cake (see page 9)

single quantity White Chocolate Ganache (see page 17)

10 inch round or square cream-colored plate

8–10 large, cream-colored, silk flowers

1 Cut the cake in half horizontally, sandwich the layers together with a little of the ganache and put the cake on the plate.

2 Use a spatula to spread the remaining ganache over the top and sides of the cake. Finish by swirling it in vertical strokes around the sides.

3 Cut the stems of the flowers down to about 2 inches. Alternatively, twist the stems under each flower so that they can be reshaped and used again. Arrange the flowers over the top of the cake.

quick tips

- The flavors of this simple cake are good enough to enjoy just as they are. However, if you want some extra zing, try using a spicy or an orange- or lemon-flavored sponge base or drizzle the cake with a coffee- or citrus-flavored liqueur before sandwiching the layers together.

- You can use delicate silk flowers to decorate the cake or more flamboyant ones—it's a matter of personal preference.

box of chocolates

serves 18

decoration time 30 minutes

7 inch square bought or homemade Rich Chocolate Cake (see page 10)

9 inch square flat plate

single quantity Dark Chocolate Ganache (see page 17)

4 x 4 oz candy bars, each 7½ x 3½ inches

1 lb selection of chocolates

5 oz chocolate truffles

5 feet chocolate-colored ribbon, about 1½ inches wide

1 Put the cake on the plate and spread the ganache over the top and sides, smoothing it into an even layer with a spatula.

2 Unwrap the candy bars and gently press a bar against each side of the cake so they meet squarely at the corners.

3 Arrange the chocolates and truffles over the top of the cake so that they resemble a layer in a box of chocolates. Wrap the ribbon around the sides of the cake, tying it in a bow.

quick tip

- Use dark or milk chocolate bars for the sides of the cake but choose thin bars rather than chunky ones. Remove them before you cut the cake into portions.

chocobloc

serves 8–10

decoration time 30 minutes

6 inch square bought or homemade Rich Chocolate Cake (see page 10)

single quantity Dark Chocolate Ganache (see page 17)

14 x 11 inch rectangular marble slab or cake board

4 tablespoons apricot jelly

plenty of gold foil (e.g., candy bar wrappings)

confectioners' sugar or cornstarch, for dusting

8 oz purple ready-to-use icing

1 Slice any dome off the top of the cake. Cut a slice 3¼ inches wide off the cake and then cut off (and discard) one-third of the slice to leave 2 rectangular pieces. Halve each horizontally and sandwich them with ganache. Put the larger cake on the marble slab or board and brush both cakes with apricot jelly.

2 While the ganache is still fairly runny, spoon a little over both cake pieces, spreading it down the sides so they are completely covered. Leave for about 10 minutes to firm up a little, then cover with the remaining ganache.

3 Transfer the chocolate bar to the marble or board and cut off a few pieces. Score the markings in the chocolate bar with a sharp knife.

4 Wrap one end of the chocolate cake in a strip of the gold foil. Dust your work surface with confectioners' sugar or cornstarch and roll out the purple icing to a rectangle, 8¾ x 5½ inches. Lay it over the cake so that one edge rests over the foil strip. Tear more foil into jagged pieces and tuck under the other end of the icing.

5 Shape the icing trimmings and a little more gold foil into "torn" wrappings and scatter them around the cake.

quick tip

- First, cover the parts of the cake that won't be hidden under icing or foil with the ganache, before it starts to thicken. Slide a piece of waxed paper under the wire rack to catch the ganache that falls through—you can scrape it up and spread it over areas of the cake that won't be visible.

chocolate truffle cake

serves 18

decoration time 30 minutes

3 x 4½ oz packages chocolate sticks

8 inch round bought or homemade
Rich Chocolate Cake (see page 10)

10–11 inch round plate

single quantity Dark Chocolate
Ganache or double quantity
Chocolate Fudge Frosting
(see page 17 or 18)

10 oz bought or homemade
chocolate truffles

2 oz pink crystallized roses

5 feet pink ribbon, 1½–2 inches wide

1 Trim the chocolate sticks so that they are ½ inch taller than the depth of the cake. Put the cake on the plate and use a spatula to spread the ganache or fudge frosting over the top and sides.

2 While the icing is still soft, secure the chocolate sticks, spacing them fractionally apart, around the sides of the cake.

3 Arrange the truffles over the top of the cake and sprinkle with roses. Tie the ribbon around the cake, finishing with a bow.

quick tip

- If you prefer to make your own chocolate truffles, heat ½ cup heavy cream in a small pan until it bubbles around the edges. Remove it from the heat and stir in 8 oz chopped dark chocolate. Leave until the chocolate has melted, then turn the mixture into a bowl and flavor it with 2 tablespoons orange or coffee liqueur, brandy, or rum. Chill until firm enough to roll into small balls and dust with cocoa powder.

confetti meringue

serves 8–10

preparation time 15 minutes

cooking time about 1¼ hours

decoration time 20 minutes

4 egg whites

1 cup superfine sugar

1¼ cups heavy cream

1 tablespoon confectioners' sugar

1–2 tablespoons rosewater

**flat round glass plate, about
10 inches in diameter**

6–8 small pink roses

**2 tablespoons bought or homemade
pink sugar crystals**

1 Line 2 cookie sheets with nonstick parchment paper. To make the meringue, beat the egg whites in a thoroughly clean bowl until stiff. Add the sugar, a tablespoon at a time, beating well after each addition until the meringue is stiff and glossy.

2 Spread a thin 8 inch circle of meringue on one cookie sheet for the base of the cake. Use 2 dessertspoons to place spoonfuls of meringue on the cookie sheets, spacing them about 1¼ inches apart. (Makes about 28 meringues.) Bake in a preheated oven, 250°F, for about 1¼ hours until the meringues are crisp, swapping the cookie sheets round halfway through cooking. Allow the meringues to cool.

3 Mix the cream with the confectioners' sugar and enough rosewater to taste, whipping them together until the mixture only just holds its shape.

4 Put the meringue circle on the serving plate. Spoon over a little of the cream, then add a circle of meringues around the edge, with 2–3 in the center. Repeat the layering, building up the meringues into a cone and finishing with a single meringue on top.

5 Pull the petals from half the roses and scatter them over the cake. Tuck the whole roses around the base of the meringues. Just before serving, dust generously with the pink sugar.

quick tip

• To make the pink sugar, put a little superfine sugar in a small bowl and add a dot of pink food coloring paste. Work the paste into the sugar with the back of a teaspoon.

frosted fruit meringue cake

serves 18

decoration time 45 minutes

3 egg whites

1 cup superfine sugar

1 fig

several small plums and apricots

10–12 cherries

½ cup blueberries

8 inch round bought or homemade Basic Sponge Cake (see page 9)

single quantity Buttercream (see page 15)

6 tablespoons raspberry or strawberry jelly

10 inch round glass plate

pinch of salt

1 Lightly beat one egg white in a small bowl until it is broken up. Put half the superfine sugar in another bowl. Using your fingers or a large paintbrush, coat the fig with egg white, then sprinkle it generously with sugar until it is evenly coated. Transfer it to a sheet of nonstick parchment paper. Frost all the remaining fruits and leave them in a cool place for at least 1 hour to dry.

2 Cut the cake horizontally into three and sandwich the layers together with the buttercream and jelly. Put the cake on a cookie sheet.

3 Beat the 2 remaining egg whites with the salt in a thoroughly clean bowl until stiff. Gradually beat in the remaining superfine sugar, a tablespoon at a time, beating well after each addition until the mixture is smooth and glossy. Use a spatula to spread a thin layer of the meringue over the top and sides of the cake to seal in any crumbs. Turn the remaining meringue onto the top of the cake and spread it over the cake evenly. Use the tip of the spatula to mark deep swirls in the meringue.

4 Bake the cake in a preheated oven, 375°F, for 5–10 minutes until the meringue is toasted. Rotate the cookie sheet once or twice during cooking to give an even color and take care that the meringue doesn't become too brown.

5 Remove the cake from the oven, transfer to the plate and leave to cool for a few minutes. Arrange the larger fruits on top of the cake, halving some of them if you like. Scatter the cherries and blueberries over the top.

quick tips

- The meringue must be made and cooked on the day you serve the cake, but you can bake the cake beforehand, sandwiching it and frosting the fruits a day in advance.

- For a special occasion, drizzle the sponge with lemon or orange liqueur before spreading it with buttercream.

vase of flowers

serves 12

preparation time 15 minutes,
plus cooling

cooking time about 45 minutes

decoration time 20 minutes

4-egg quantity Basic Sponge Cake
mixture (see page 9)

double quantity Buttercream
(see page 15)

square plate

confectioners' sugar or cornstarch,
for dusting

1½ lb dark red ready-to-use icing

small bunch of dried roses

plenty of raffia

1 Turn the cake mixture into a greased and lined cake pan, 8 inches square, and level the surface. Bake in a preheated oven, 325°F, for about 45 minutes or until just firm, and a tester, inserted in the center, comes out clean. Allow to cool.

2 Slice the domed surface off the top of the cake and cut it into 4 equal pieces. Use half the buttercream to stack the cakes together. Transfer the cake to the plate and spread the remaining buttercream over the top and sides with a spatula.

3 Dust your work surface with confectioners' sugar or cornstarch and roll out the red icing. Cut out 4 rectangles, each ½ inch longer than the depth of the cake and 4½ inches wide. Position a rectangle against each side of the cake, dampening the edges with a paintbrush so they stick together.

4 Cut the rose stems to 2 inches long and wrap the ends in plastic wrap or foil. Press them into the top of the cake. Allow the icing to harden for a couple of hours or overnight, then wrap the raffia loosely around the sides.

quick tip

• Serving a tall cake like this can be awkward. It will be easier if you remove the raffia and flowers first and then split the cake in half horizontally so that you can serve the halves cut into squares.

feathered hat

serves 12

decoration time 30 minutes

6 inch round bought or homemade Basic Sponge Cakes (see page 9)

single quantity Buttercream (see page 15)

6 tablespoons smooth raspberry or strawberry jelly

11 inch round cake board

confectioners' sugar or cornstarch, for dusting

2 lb ivory-colored ready-to-use icing

20 inches bottle green wired ribbon, about 3 inches wide

spray of dark green feathers

large ivory-colored silk flower

ivory-colored ribbon for edge of cake board

1 Cut a slice off the top of each cake so they are about 2 inches deep. Cut each cake in half horizontally and sandwich the 4 layers together with half the buttercream and all the jelly. Position the cake to one side of the cake board and spread the remaining buttercream over the top and sides.

2 Dust your work surface with confectioners' sugar or cornstarch and roll out 1½ lb of the ivory-colored icing to a circle, 11 inches across. Lift it over the cake and smooth the icing down the sides. Trim off any excess around the base.

3 Dampen the board with a little water. Combine the trimmings with the remaining icing and use it to cover the cake board. The easiest way to do this is to roll out the icing into a thick, curved crescent shape, roughly the same size as the exposed board area. Trim the inner curve of the crescent and lift the icing around the cake, smoothing it out to fit the board and trimming off the excess around the edges.

4 Make a loop in the center of the green ribbon and tuck it to one side of the cake, bending the wired ends of the ribbon over the cake. Secure it to the iced board with clear adhesive tape. Position the feathers and silk flower against the side of the cake, pressing them gently into the icing. Secure the ivory-colored ribbon around the edge of the cake board.

quick tip

- This makes a great birthday cake for a friend who's crazy about hats. Use any color theme for the icing and decorations, which can be as traditional or as flamboyant as you like.

green thumb

serves 20

decoration time 30 minutes, plus drying

2 oz purple ready-to-use icing

2 toothpicks

2 oz gray ready-to-use icing

9 inch round bought or homemade Basic Sponge Cake (see page 9)

single quantity Buttercream (see page 15)

6 tablespoons smooth raspberry or strawberry jelly

12–14 inch round wooden board

small terra-cotta pot, about 2½ inches in diameter

4 oz dark chocolate, finely grated

confectioners' sugar or cornstarch, for dusting

2 lb green ready-to-use icing

1 small sprig of bay leaves

plenty of small sprigs of lavender leaves and flowers

1 Make the trowel by rolling the purple icing into a thick sausage. Flatten the ends and use the back of a small knife to indent markings at each end. Press 2 toothpicks, slightly apart, into one end. Flatten the gray icing into a scoop shape with one straight edge. Press the toothpicks into the straight edge and rest the trowel over a foil-covered rolling pin to harden for about 24 hours.

2 Cut the cake in half horizontally and sandwich the layers with all but 1 tablespoon of the buttercream and half the jelly. Put it on the board. Use a spoon to scoop out a little of the center of the cake and pack it into the pot. Spread it with the reserved buttercream and sprinkle with a little of the grated chocolate. Scoop out a little more of the cake to make a wider cavity. Spread the remaining jelly over the top and sides of the cake.

3 Dust your work surface with confectioners' sugar or cornstarch and roll out the green icing to a circle, 14 inches across. Lay the icing over the cake, easing it into the cavity and around the sides and letting the excess icing rest on the board.

4 Press the bay and a few lavender sprigs into the cake in the pot. Arrange more sprigs around the sides of the cake, securing them in the icing on the board.

5 Scatter a pile of grated chocolate over the top of the cake and in piles around the sides. Position the pot and trowel on top of the cake.

quick tip

• Herbs and herb flowers make pretty decorations and won't wilt as quickly as other fresh flowers, so if you use them you can assemble the cake a day in advance. Alternatively, use other small flowers, such as rose buds, primroses, or geraniums, and position them at the last minute.

golfer's bag

serves 16

decoration time 30 minutes,
plus drying

12 oz white ready-to-use icing

**5 x 6 inch lengths wood or
plastic doweling**

½ oz red ready-to-use icing

**confectioners' sugar or cornstarch,
for dusting**

5 oz green ready-to-use icing

9 inch round cake board

**2 x 6 inch round bought or
homemade Basic Sponge Cakes
(see page 9)**

**single quantity Buttercream
(see page 15)**

3 tablespoons smooth apricot jelly

2 lb brown ready-to-use icing

1 tube black decorator frosting

silver food coloring

red ribbon for edge of cake board

1 Roll 5 balls, each 1 oz, of white icing and gently indent each with the end of a paintbrush to make golf balls. Shape the heads of 5 clubs, each 1½ oz, in white icing, adding markings with a knife. Dampen the tips of the doweling rods and press them into the ends. Shape several small tees in red icing. Leave them with the clubs and golf balls on a sheet of nonstick parchment paper to dry overnight.

2 Dust your work surface with confectioners' sugar or cornstarch and roll out the green icing. Use it to cover the cake board, trimming off the excess.

3 Cut the cakes in half horizontally and sandwich them together with the buttercream. Put the stacked cakes on the board and spread the jelly over the top and sides.

4 Reserve 4 oz of the brown icing. Roll out a further 4 oz of the brown icing to a circle, 6 inches diameter, and lay it over the top cake. Roll out the remainder and cut out a rectangle, 20 x 6½ inches. Dampen the short edges and wrap it around the cake so that the top edge is about ¾ inch higher than the cakes. Smooth the join together.

5 Roll out the reserved brown icing and cut out a rectangle, 5 x 4 inches. Dampen the edges and secure it to the bag for a pocket. Cut out a strip, 6 x ¾ inch, and secure the ends to the bag for a handle.

6 Use the decorator frosting to pipe stitches over the bag. Arrange the golf balls and tees beside it.

7 Paint the clubs and rods with silver food coloring and leave to dry. Press them gently into the top of the cake and paint the backs. Secure the ribbon around the edge of the board.

quick tip

- Wood or plastic doweling rods are available from cake-decorating stores and from hardware stores. If you buy long sticks, cut them to size before using.

triple chocolate cupcakes

makes 12

decoration time 20 minutes

4 oz white chocolate, chopped

4 oz milk chocolate, chopped

4 oz dark chocolate, chopped

3 tablespoons unsalted butter

12 bought or homemade chocolate Cupcakes (see page 13)

cocoa powder, for dusting

1 Put the white, milk, and dark chocolate in separate bowls and add 1 tablespoon butter to each. Melt all the chocolate, either one at a time in the microwave or by resting each bowl over a saucepan of gently simmering water. Stir occasionally until melted and smooth.

2 Use a small spatula to spread the melted white chocolate over 4 of the cakes and sprinkle with a little cocoa powder.

3 Put 2 tablespoons of the melted milk and dark chocolate in separate pastry bags fitted with writing tips. Spread the milk chocolate over 4 more of the cakes and pipe dots of dark chocolate over the milk chocolate.

4 Spread the dark chocolate over the 4 remaining cakes and scribble with lines of piped milk chocolate.

quick tip

• When you melt chocolate in a bowl over hot water, break the chocolate into small pieces and put it in an ovenproof bowl that will stand above the water. Take care that steam from the water doesn't condense in the bowl—even a few drops of water will spoil the chocolate.

chocolate caramel cupcakes

makes 12

cooking time 5 minutes

decoration time 15 minutes

⅔ **cup sweetened condensed milk**

¼ **cup superfine sugar**

⅓ **cup unsalted butter**

2 **tablespoons corn syrup**

12 **bought or homemade Cupcakes (see page 13)**

4 **oz dark chocolate, chopped**

4 **oz milk chocolate, chopped**

1 Put the condensed milk, sugar, butter, and corn syrup in a medium heavy saucepan and heat gently, stirring, until the sugar dissolves. Cook over a gentle heat, stirring, for about 5 minutes until the mixture has turned a pale fudge color.

2 Leave the caramel to cool for 2 minutes then spoon over the top of the cakes.

3 Melt the dark and milk chocolate in separate heatproof bowls, either one at a time in the microwave or by resting each bowl over a saucepan of gently simmering water. Put a couple of teaspoons of each type of melted chocolate onto a cake, mixing up the colors, and tap the cake on the work surface to level the chocolate. Use the tip of a cocktail stick or fine tester to swirl the chocolates together to marble them slightly. Repeat on the remaining cakes.

quick tip

• For a really quick teatime treat, use the caramel and chocolate topping on a plain bought sponge cake.

florentine cupcakes

makes 12

cooking time 8 minutes

decoration time 10 minutes

¾ cup slivered almonds

⅓ cup golden raisins

1 cup candied cherries, quartered

4 tablespoons corn syrup

12 bought or homemade Cupcakes
(see page 13)

2 oz dark chocolate, broken
into pieces

1 Mix together the slivered almonds, golden raisins, candied cherries and corn syrup in a bowl. Tip the mixture onto a greased cookie sheet and spread in a thin layer. Bake in a preheated oven, 400°F, for 8 minutes or until the nuts and syrup are turning golden. Remove from the oven and leave to cool slightly.

2 Break up the mixture and scatter it over the cakes in an even layer.

3 Melt the chocolate in a heatproof bowl, either in the microwave or by resting the bowl over a saucepan of gently simmering water. Put the melted chocolate in a pastry bag fitted with a writing tip. Scribble lines of chocolate across the fruit and nut topping. Leave to set.

quick tips

• Instead of slivered almonds use a mixture of chopped nuts, if you prefer, or walnuts and almonds, finely chopped.

• Replace ¼ cup of the candied cherries with chopped candied rind.

white chocolate curl cakes

makes 12

decoration time 15 minutes

4 oz chunky piece white chocolate

single quantity white Chocolate
Fudge Frosting (see page 18)

12 bought or homemade white
chocolate chip Cupcake
(see page 13)

confectioners' sugar, for dusting

1 Use a vegetable peeler to pare curls from
the chocolate. If the chocolate breaks off
in small, brittle shards, try softening it in the
microwave for a few seconds first, but take care
not to overheat and melt it. Set the curls aside
in a cool place while you ice the cakes.

2 Use a small spatula to spread the fudge
frosting all over the tops of the cakes.

3 Pile the chocolate curls onto the cakes and
dust them with confectioners' sugar.

quick tip

- Make chocolate flakes instead of curls by
  using the coarsest side of a grater.

strawberry creams

makes 12

decoration time 20 minutes

**12 bought or homemade Cupcakes
(see page 13)**

2 cups small strawberries

⅔ cup heavy cream

2 teaspoons superfine sugar

½ teaspoon vanilla extract

4 tablespoons redcurrant jelly

1 tablespoon water

1 Use a small sharp knife to scoop out the center of each cake to leave a deep cavity. Reserve 6 of the smallest strawberries and thinly slice the remainder.

2 Use a hand-held electric beater to whip the cream with the sugar and vanilla extract until just peaking. Spoon a little into the center of each cake and flatten slightly with the back of the spoon.

3 Arrange the sliced strawberries, overlapping, around the edges of each cake. Halve the reserved strawberries and put a strawberry half in the center of each cake.

4 Heat the redcurrant jelly in a small heavy saucepan with the water until melted, then brush over the strawberries using a pastry brush. Store the cakes in a cool place until ready to serve.

quick tips

- Raspberries will be a delicious alternative to strawberries.

- If you use a fruit such as apricots or nectarines, use apricot jelly instead of redcurrant jelly to glaze the cakes.

stars, spots, and stripes

makes 12

decoration time 20 minutes

½ quantity Buttercream (see page 15)

12 bought or homemade Cupcakes (see page 13)

confectioners' sugar or cornstarch, for dusting

5 oz white ready-to-use icing

4 oz blue ready-to-use icing

1 Use a small spatula to spread the buttercream in a thin layer over the tops of the cakes.

2 Dust your work surface with confectioners' sugar or cornstarch and knead the ready-to-use icings, keeping the colors separate. Take 2 oz of the white icing, roll it out thinly and cut out 4 circles with a plain 2½ inch cookie cutter. Use a tiny star-shaped cutter to cut out 6 small stars from each circle. Thinly roll out a little of the blue icing and cut out stars. Fit the blue stars into each white round and carefully transfer to 4 of the cakes.

3 Thinly roll out another 2 oz of the white icing. Roll balls of blue icing, about the size of a small pea, between the finger and thumb. Press at intervals onto the white icing. Gently roll the icing with a rolling pin so the blue icing forms dots over the white. Cut out 4 circles with a plain cookie cutter and transfer to 4 more of the cakes.

4 From the remaining blue and white icing cut out long strips, ¼ inch wide, and lay them together on the work surface to make stripes. Roll lightly with a rolling pin to flatten them and secure together, then cut out 4 more circles. Position them on top of the remaining 4 cakes.

quick tip

- The same technique of cutting out shapes from one color and filling them with the same shapes cut from a different color can be used for numbers, to make these little cakes suitable for birthday parties.

butterfly cakes

makes 12

decoration time 15 minutes

**12 bought or homemade Cupcakes
(see page 13)**

**single quantity Buttercream
(see page 15)**

1 Use a small, sharp knife to cut out the center from each cake and slice each scooped-out piece in half.

2 Put the buttercream in a big pastry bag fitted with a large star tip. Pipe a large swirl of icing into the hollow of each cake.

3 Reposition the cut-out centers on each cake at an angle of 45 degrees so they resemble butterfly wings.

quick tip

- For a special occasion, flavor the buttercream with chocolate or citrus and dust the cakes with confectioners' sugar.

piped shell cakes

makes 12

decoration time 30 minutes

1½ cups confectioners' sugar, plus a little extra

1–2 tablespoons lemon or orange juice

12 bought or homemade Cupcakes (see page 13)

½ quantity Buttercream (see page 15)

pink and lilac food colorings

1 Mix the confectioners' sugar in a bowl with 1 tablespoon of the lemon or orange juice. Gradually add the remaining juice, stirring well with a wooden spoon until the icing holds its shape but is not difficult to spread. You might not need all the juice.

2 Reserve 3 tablespoons of the icing and use a small spatula to spread the remainder over the tops of the cakes. Stir a little extra confectioners' sugar into the reserved icing to thicken it until it just forms peaks when lifted with a knife. Transfer the icing to a pastry bag fitted with a writing tip.

3 Color half the buttercream with pink food coloring and the other half with lilac. Transfer the icing to separate pastry bags fitted with star tips.

4 Pipe rows of pink, lilac, and white icing across the cakes.

quick tip

- Children love piping their own designs and personalizing cakes with names or messages. The pink and lilac piping looks pretty on the white background, but you can choose any mixture of colors you like.

3
time to celebrate

first prize

serves 24

decoration time about 1 hour

9 inch square bought or homemade Basic Sponge Cake (see page 9)

single quantity Buttercream (see page 15)

6 tablespoons smooth strawberry or raspberry jelly

18–12 inch rectangular cake board or tray

2½ lb white ready-to-use icing

confectioners' sugar or cornstarch, for dusting

2 oz brown ready-to-use icing

8 oz gray ready-to-use icing

black food coloring

gold food coloring

36 inches red ribbon, about 1¼ inches wide

red rosette

red ribbon for edges of cake board

1 Slice any dome off the top of the cake. Using a ruler as a guide, cut the cake vertically in half. Cut each half into 3 equal vertical slices and lay the slices together on their sides to make one large rectangle. Cut horizontally through the whole rectangle. Use the buttercream and half the jelly to sandwich the cakes together, reassembling them in the rectangle on the board. Spread the remaining jelly over the top and sides of the cake.

2 Reserve 8 oz of the white icing. Dust your work surface with confectioners' sugar or cornstarch and roll out the remainder of the white icing to a rectangle that will cover the cake. Lift it over the cake, easing it down the sides. Trim off the excess around the base.

3 Make the trophy by rolling out the brown icing to a rectangle, 3 x 2 inches, and put it on the top of the cake for the trophy stand, using a dampened paintbrush to secure it in position. Cut out a square of waxed paper, 4 x 4 inches, and round off 2 corners to make the shape of a goblet.

4 Roll out a small piece of gray icing and cut out a trophy base, about 2 inches deep and with curved sides. Secure it to the stand. Using the waxed paper shape as a template, cut out the goblet shape and secure in position. Roll out the remaining gray icing under the palms of your hands into thin ropes and bend them into handles and trimmings for the trophy base.

5 Lightly knead dots of black food coloring into the reserved white icing to make a marbled effect. Use this to cover the edges of the cake board, trimming off the excess around the edges.

6 Use the gold food coloring to add highlights to the trophy and stand. Secure the ribbon around the sides of the cake and position the rosette beside one of the handles. Secure more ribbon around the edges of the cake board.

quick tips

- Cut the cake into perfectly even thicknesses to make a good base for the icing.

- Serve at a celebration for any sporting triumph—tennis, swimming, golf, or horse-riding—and use the appropriate team colors. Paint names or a message on the stand.

graduation cake

serves 20

preparation time 15 minutes

cooking time 1–1¼ hours

decoration time 1 hour

6-egg quantity Basic Sponge Cake mixture (see page 9)

single quantity Buttercream (see page 15)

3 tablespoons smooth apricot jelly

8 oz ivory-colored ready-to-use icing

confectioners' sugar or cornstarch, for dusting

2 lb purple ready-to-use icing

12 x 10 inch wooden board

2 oz yellow ready-to-use icing

3 oz chocolate brown ready-to-use icing

1 tube yellow decorator frosting

gold food coloring

1 Turn the cake mixture into a greased and lined cake pan, 9 inches square. Bake in a preheated oven, 325°F, for 1–1¼ hours until just firm and a tester inserted into the center comes out clean. Allow to cool. Slice any dome off the top of the cake. Cut a slice, 2 inches wide, off one side and position it at one end of the larger piece. Trim off the excess to make a rectangle. Cut the cake in half horizontally and sandwich the layers with the buttercream, securing the smaller piece of cake to the larger one with more buttercream.

2 Use a sharp knife to round off the corners of one long side. Cut curves into the other long side and the ends to make a book shape. Spread the 3 curved sides with a little jelly. Reserve a little of the ivory-colored icing. Dust your work surface with confectioners' sugar or cornstarch and roll out the remainder of the icing to a long strip the depth of the cake and the length of the 3 sides. Press it into position and score it with a knife.

3 Roll out a scant half of the purple icing to a rectangle about ½ inch longer and ½ inch wider than the cake. Put it on the board and position the cake on top so that the ivory-colored icing sits about ¼ inch away from the edges of the purple icing. Roll out the remaining purple icing to the same length but add an extra 2 inches to the width to cover the "spine" of the book. Position it on the cake, tucking the ends under the spine.

4 Use the reserved ivory-colored icing to make the owl's head and body and secure to the cake with a dampened paintbrush. Use the yellow icing for eyes and claws and the brown icing for wings, the top of the head, the beak, and centers of the eyes. Position 2 more rectangles of brown icing on the spine. Pipe yellow icing around the edges and spine and around the owl's wings. Dab spots of gold food coloring on the owl's breast.

quick tip

• Purple icing can be made by kneading Grape Violet food coloring into white icing or by kneading together red and blue icings.

bon voyage

serves 20

decoration time 30 minutes

9 inch square bought or homemade Basic Sponge Cake (see page 9)

single quantity Buttercream (see page 15)

large metal tray or 11 inch square cake board

3 tablespoons smooth apricot jelly

confectioners' sugar or cornstarch, for dusting

2 lb dark red ready-to-use icing

8 oz white ready-to-use icing

silver food coloring

1 Slice any dome off the top of the cake. Cut a slice 3¼ inches wide off the cake and then cut off (and discard) one-third of the slice to leave 2 rectangular pieces. Halve each horizontally and sandwich the layers with buttercream. Put the larger cake on the tray or board and brush both cakes with apricot jelly.

2 Dust your work surface with confectioners' sugar or cornstarch and roll out two-thirds of the red icing to a rectangle, 4 inches longer and wider than the large cake. Lay the icing over the cake, smoothing the icing down the sides and trimming off the excess around the base. Cover the small cake with the remaining red icing and put it on the large cake.

3 Roll out a thin strip of white icing and trim it to a strip ½ inch wide and long enough to go around the small cake. Lightly dampen the back of the strip and secure it in position. Use a larger strip to wrap around the large cake. Run the tip of a knife along each strip to make an indentation. Cut out small rectangles of icing and position 2 rectangles on the small case at either side of the strip and 2 on the large case. Add smaller rectangles of icing for the clasps.

4 Roll 2 pieces of icing, each 1½ oz, into sausage shapes and bend the ends over to shape handles. Secure them in position. Paint the clasps with silver food coloring.

quick tips

- If you're throwing a large party for someone about to set off on their travels, you could use a rich fruit cake instead of a sponge cake. If you do, cover it with almond paste before icing (see page 21).

- As a finishing touch, write the recipient's name and destination on a luggage label and attach it to one of the handles.

welcome home

serves 40

decoration time 1 hour

10 inch round Rich Fruit Cake, covered with almond paste (see pages 11 and 21 for recipe and technique)

12 inch round cake board

confectioners' sugar or cornstarch, for dusting

2 lb white ready-to-use icing

3 oz each of orange, chocolate brown, green, red, and blue ready-to-use icing

1 tube red decorator frosting

red ribbon for edge of cake board

1 Put the cake on the board. Dust your work surface with confectioners' sugar or cornstarch and roll out the white icing to a circle, 15 inches across. Lay it over the cake, smoothing the icing around the sides and trimming off the excess around the base.

2 Roll out a little of the orange icing and trim to a rectangle, 15 x 2¾ inches. Dampen the underside lightly with water and put it on top of the cake. Roll out the brown icing and cut out 2 strips, ¼ inch wide and each the width of the orange rectangle. Position one strip at each end of the orange icing. Cut out 2 further rectangles, 6½ x 1¼ inches, from the brown icing. Lay them against the long sides of the orange icing and trim off the ends at angles to represent open doors. Cut out windows in the top half of the doors and add 2 doorknobs.

3 Pipe scallops of red decorator frosting around the sides of the cake and at the top of the doors. Thinly roll out a little orange, green, red, and blue icing and cut them into strips ¾ inch wide. From each strip cut out triangles for bunting. Dampen the pieces with water and secure them to the cake. Use red icing to cover the edges of the cake board.

4 Shape a small case in blue icing and put it on top of the cake next to the open doors. Write a message on the bunting if desired and secure the red ribbon around the edge of the board.

quick tips

- Use the decorator frosting tube to write a message—the recipient's name or "Welcome," for example—on the bunting on top of the cake.

- If you're not used to writing with icing, practice on a sheet of waxed paper.

new parents

serves 24

decoration time 1 hour

6 inch and 8 inch round bought or
homemade Basic Sponge Cakes
(see page 9)

double quantity Buttercream
(see page 15)

8 tablespoons lemon or orange curd

10–11 inch round or square plate

confectioners' sugar or cornstarch,
for dusting

2¾ lb pale pink or blue
ready-to-use icing

1 oz flesh-colored ready-to-use icing

2 oz dark pink or blue
ready-to-use icing

blue food coloring

2 oz white ready-to-use icing

2 oz yellow ready-to-use icing

small plastic cake decorations
(e.g., diaper pins, rattles)

2 oz small pink and yellow
soft candies

1 Cut each cake in half horizontally and sandwich the layers together with half the buttercream and the lemon or orange curd. Spread the remaining buttercream over the top and sides of the cakes. Put the larger cake on the plate.

2 Dust your work surface with confectioners' sugar or cornstarch and roll out two-thirds of the pink or blue icing to a circle, 13 inches across, and cover the larger cake, smoothing the icing down the sides and trimming off the excess around the base. Roll out the remaining icing to a circle, 11 inches across, and cover the smaller cake. Position the smaller cake on the center of the larger one.

3 Roll a small ball of flesh-colored icing for baby's head, adding a small button nose. Shape hands and feet with more flesh-colored icing. Roll the dark pink or blue icing into an oval and flatten it slightly with the palm of your hand. Make 2 cuts for the arms and one for the legs. Smooth out the edges and cut off the tips. Make button markings with the tip of a paintbrush. Secure the baby to the top of the cake with a dampened paintbrush, bending the shape into a sitting-up position.

4 Secure the head, hands, and feet and add features with the blue coloring and a fine paintbrush.

5 Shape feeding bottles from the remaining icing and secure them around the cake with the plastic cake decorations. Scatter plenty of small candies around the tiers.

quick tip

• This makes a fabulous gift for new parents, who can indulge in it themselves or serve it to the stream of visitors who'll come to admire their baby. It would also make a good christening cake if you're looking for something a bit different.

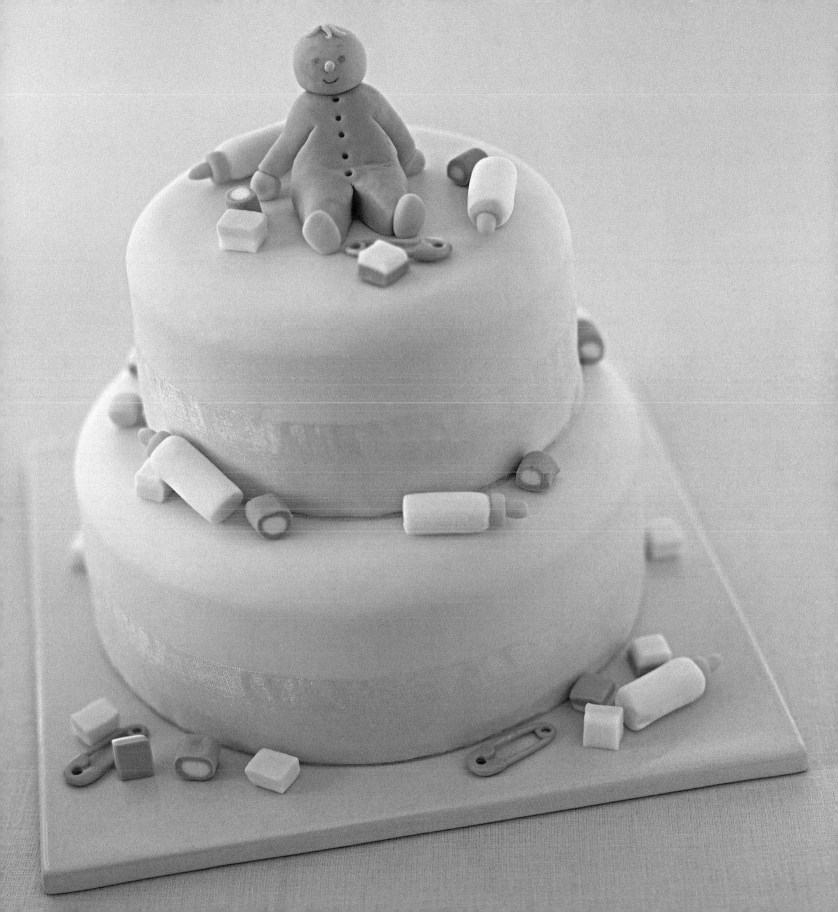

first night

serves 24

decoration time 1 hour, plus drying

confectioners' sugar or cornstarch,
for dusting

2½ lb white ready-to-use icing

10 inch round bought or homemade
Basic Sponge Cake (see page 9)

single quantity Buttercream
(see page 15)

6 tablespoons raspberry or
strawberry jelly

12--14 inch round plate, preferably
gold or red

14 oz red ready-to-use icing

20 inches fine red cord

20 inches fine gold cord

2 oz purple ready-to-use icing

gold food coloring

1 Wrap a piece of nonstick parchment paper around a tall tumbler and prop it up at either side with a little icing. To make the mask templates cut out 2 rectangles, each 4 x 3 inches, from waxed paper and fold them in half lengthwise. Round off the lower half of the masks from halfway along the sides to the point of the folded edge. Gently curve the top edge of the masks from the folded point to the sides. Cut out eyes. Cut a smiling mouth on one mask and a sad mouth on the other.

2 Dust your work surface with confectioners' sugar or cornstarch and roll out 4 oz of the white icing. Lay the templates over the icing and cut out the mask shapes. Carefully transfer them to the tumbler so they set in a curved shape. Leave them for 24 hours.

3 Cut the cake in half horizontally and sandwich the layers with half the buttercream and all the jelly. Put it on the plate and spread the top and sides with the remaining buttercream.

4 Roll out the remaining white icing to a circle, 14 inches across, and cover the cake, smoothing the icing around the sides and trimming off the excess around the base.

5 Halve the red icing and thinly roll one half to a rectangle, about 11 x 5 inches. Drape the icing over one side of the cake, pinching it together slightly in the center to resemble curtains. Use a dampened paintbrush to secure the red icing to the white so it doesn't slip. Secure 2 lengths of cord around the icing then make the other curtain in the same way. Cut out thin strips of purple icing, about ¼ inch wide, and secure them around the edges of the curtains.

6 Carefully peel the paper away from the masks and paint them gold. Position them, slightly overlapping, on top of the cake.

quick tip

- This is a brilliant cake for budding actors. The masks are far easier to make than they look and can be made well in advance so they have plenty of time to harden. Make a spare one of each—just in case of breakages.

winter wedding cake

serves 50–55

decoration time 1 hour, plus drying

6 inch and 10 inch round bought or homemade Rich Fruit Cakes, covered with almond paste (see pages 11 and 21 for recipe and technique)

14–16 inch round glass plate or cake stand

double quantity Royal Icing (see page 18)

1 egg white, lightly beaten

12 rosemary sprigs, about 2½ inches long

8 bay leaf sprigs

superfine and confectioners' sugar, for dusting

8 small fir cones

1 cup sugar cubes

6 tea lights

1 Put the larger cake on the plate and spread two-thirds of the royal icing over it, swirling it in an even layer with a spatula. Put the smaller cake on top and cover it with the remaining icing.

2 To frost the herb sprigs, put the lightly beaten egg white in a bowl. Use your fingers to coat a rosemary sprig with egg white so that it's evenly moistened but not dripping. Dip the sprig into superfine sugar and transfer it to a tray covered with nonstick parchment paper. Allow it to dry for at least 1 hour. Coat the remaining rosemary and the bay leaf sprigs in the same way.

3 Using a tea strainer, generously dust the fir cones with confectioners' sugar. Put the sugar cubes into a plastic bag and tap them gently with a rolling pin until they are broken into smaller pieces.

4 Dust the plate with confectioners' sugar. Position 2 tea lights on the top tier and 4 on the lower tier. Arrange the herbs and fir cones around the tea lights and scatter the pieces of sugar to fill the gaps between the decorations and around the lower tier. Cover loosely and store in a cool place for up to 1 week.

quick tip

• **This cake will make a great centerpiece for your Christmas table or for a winter wedding anniversary or birthday party. Don't forget to light the tea lights for a truly stunning effect!**

white chocolate wedding cake

serves 30–35

decoration time 1½ hours

13 oz white chocolate

2 tablespoons unsalted butter

6 inch and 10 inch round bought or homemade Rich Chocolate Cakes (see page 10)

12–14 inch round glass or frosted glass plate

triple quantity White Chocolate Ganache (see page 17)

12–14 white freesias

8–10 white or coral pink ranunculus

6–8 white or cream-colored lisianthus

1 Break the white chocolate into pieces and put them in a bowl with the butter. Place the bowl over a saucepan of gently simmering water and leave it until the chocolate has melted. Gently stir the chocolate to incorporate the butter. Tip the mixture onto a piece of marble or glass or a thoroughly clean plastic cutting board and spread it to a thin, even layer. Leave in a cool place or in the refrigerator until set.

2 When the chocolate is just set, draw a fine-bladed knife across it at an angle of 45 degrees to pare off long chocolate curls. If the chocolate breaks off in brittle shavings it's too cold, so leave it at room temperature for a few minutes and try again. If the chocolate is sticky and clings to the knife put it in the refrigerator for about 10 minutes and then try again.

3 Put the larger cake on the plate and spread two-thirds of the ganache over it. While the ganache is still soft press the chocolate curls vertically into it. You needn't be too precise or careful about doing this—the more casually it's done, the better the finished result.

4 Position the small cake on top of the larger one and cover it with the remaining ganache. Press more chocolate curls around the sides. Keep the cake in a cool place or in the refrigerator until ready to serve.

5 Cut the stems of all the flowers short and use them to decorate the tops of the cakes.

quick tips

- Chocolate curls—caraque—are stunning cake decorations and are easy to make once you've got the hang of the technique. Make them a couple of weeks in advance and keep them in a cool place or in the refrigerator until you need them.

- The day before the wedding, complete the cake up to the end of step 4, leaving only the flowers to arrange on the day.

chocolate wedding cake

serves 34

decoration time 1½ hours

6 inch round and 10 inch round bought or homemade Rich Chocolate Cakes (see page 10)

triple quantity Chocolate Fudge Frosting (see page 18)

8 inch, 12 inch, 13 inch, and 14 inch round cake boards

confectioners' sugar or cornstarch, for dusting

4 lb chocolate brown ready-to-use icing

5 feet coffee-colored ribbon, 1½ inches wide

13 feet white ribbon for edges of cake boards

1 lb box of chocolates

4 oz mixed chocolate coffee beans

1 Cut both cakes in half horizontally and sandwich the layers together with half the chocolate fudge frosting. Put the smaller cake on the 8 inch board and the larger cake on the 12 inch board. Spread the top and sides of the cakes with the remaining frosting.

2 Dust your work surface with confectioners' sugar or cornstarch and roll out 2 lb of the icing to a circle, 14 inches across. Lift the icing over the larger cake. Smooth the icing down the sides and trim off the excess around the base. Reserve the trimmings.

3 Roll out a further 1½ lb of the icing and use it to cover the smaller cake. Knead the trimmings and remaining icing together. Secure the 2 largest cake boards together with clear adhesive tape, then secure the large cake, on its board, on top.

4 Cover all the top edges of the cake boards with the remaining icing, starting with the smallest and working down to the largest board. Rest the smaller cake on top of the larger one. Wrap the coffee-colored ribbon around the cakes. Secure the ivory-colored ribbon around all the boards.

5 Pile the chocolates on top of the smaller cake and around the edge of the larger one. Scatter the coffee beans on top.

quick tip

• If you're transporting this cake to a special event keep the tiers separate until you get there and assemble the cake in its final position, scattering over the chocolates and coffee beans at the last minute.

ribbony chocolate wedding cake

serves 50

decoration time 1 hour, plus standing

6 inch, 8 inch, and 10 inch round bought or homemade Rich Chocolate Cakes (see page 10)

triple quantity Dark Chocolate Ganache (see page 17)

12 inch round cake stand or glass plate

10 feet wired red ribbon, about 1½ inches wide

10 feet wired lilac or cream-colored ribbon, about 1 inch wide

about 20 small, dried, red, pale green, lilac, or cream-colored flowers

1 Cut each cake in half horizontally and use about a quarter of the ganache to sandwich the layers together.

2 Put the largest cake on the cake stand or plate and cover it with a scant half of the ganache, swirling it in an even layer with a spatula. Rest the medium-size cake on top and spread with more ganache. Position the smallest cake on top and spread with the remaining ganache. Leave the cake in a cool place for about 1 hour until the chocolate has firmed up slightly.

3 Wrap the red ribbon around your hand and then uncoil it loosely around the cake, starting at the top and working around the cake in a spiral to the bottom. Pressing the edge of the ribbon gently into the chocolate icing on the top tier should be sufficient to hold it in place. It can then be secured under the edge of the cake stand at the other end with a small piece of clear adhesive tape.

4 Create the same effect with the narrower ribbon, keeping the coil loose and informal.

5 Tuck the flowers, in groups of 2–3, among the coils of ribbon decoration.

quick tips

- Before covering the cake layers with ganache, drizzle them with an orange or coffee liqueur or with brandy. Allow about 4 tablespoons for the top tier, ½ cup for the middle tier, and ⅔ cup for the bottom tier.

- If you want to make the cake in advance, assemble it to the end of step 2 and store overnight in a cool place. Add the flowers and ribbons the following day.

layered rose wedding cake

serves 75–80

decoration time 1½ hours

5 inch, 7 inch, and 9 inch square
bought or homemade Rich Fruit
Cakes, covered with almond paste
(see pages 11 and 21 for recipe
and technique)

6 inch, 8 inch, and 11 inch square
cake boards, plus 3 x 5 inch and
3 x 7 inch round boards for stacking

confectioners' sugar or cornstarch,
for dusting

5 lb ivory-colored ready-to-use icing

10 feet ivory-colored ribbon for
edges of boards

about 30 pale pink or
30 ivory-colored open roses or
a mixture of the 2 colors

small posy of roses for top of cake

1 Put the cakes on the square boards. Dust your work surface with confectioners' sugar or cornstarch and roll out 2 lb of the icing to a 14 inch square. Lift the icing over the largest cake. Smooth it down the sides and trim off the excess around the base.

2 Cover the medium-size cake with 1½ lb of the icing and the small cake with the remainder, each time rolling the icing to a square 5 inches larger than the diameter of the cake.

3 Use clear adhesive tape to fasten together the 5 inch boards and the 7 inch boards. Secure the ivory-colored ribbon around the edges of the boards.

4 To assemble the cake put the 7 inch stacked cake boards on the large cake and position the medium-size cake on top. Put the 5 inch stacked cake boards on top of this and position the small cake on top.

5 Cut the rose stems down to ¾ inch. Tuck all the roses, closely together, around the 2 bottom tiers, fitting them together so they make an attractive decoration without looking too crammed. Arrange the posy of roses on top of the cake.

quick tip

• This cake can be prepared up to the end of step 4 several weeks in advance, but the assembly of the roses needs to be done on the day. Set the posy in a shallow bowl of water and wrap the ends of the other roses in moistened cotton batting, then in foil or clingfilm so the water does not seep out over the cake.

sugared almond wedding cake

serves 20

decoration time 30 minutes

7 inch square homemade Rich Fruit Cake (see page 11) or 3 bought fruit slab cakes

4 tablespoons smooth apricot jelly

10 inch square or 12 inch round cake plate or cake stand

confectioners' sugar or cornstarch, for dusting

3 lb white ready-to-use icing

7 inch square silver cake board

2 lb white or colored sugar coated almonds

6 feet wired ribbon, about 2 inches wide

silver, pink, or white wedding confetti

1 Spread the top and sides of the cake with the apricot jelly. If you are using bought cakes, secure them together with a little of the jelly to make a deep, square cake. Put the cake on the plate or cake stand.

2 Dust your work surface with confectioners' sugar or cornstarch and knead the icing to soften it slightly. Roll out 7 oz to a 7 inch square, and lay it on top of the cake. Reserve 9 oz of the remaining icing and roll out the remainder to a rectangle, 12 x 8 inches. From this cut out 4 rectangles, each 7 inches long and ½ inch deeper than the cake. Make sure that all 4 rectangles are the same length and depth. Secure a rectangle to each cake side, pinching them together at the corners to secure.

3 Dampen the top and sides of the cake board with water. Roll out the remaining icing to a 9 inch square and use it to cover the board, folding the icing down the sides and pinching it together at the corners. Trim off the excess around the base and at the corners.

4 Scatter the sugared almonds into the top of the cake and carefully balance the icing-covered "lid" in position. Cut the ribbon into 4 even lengths. Use the tip of a knife to ease one end of each length under each side of the cake. Bring the loose ends up over the top of the cake and fasten them together in a loose bow. Scatter the base with the confetti.

quick tips

- Don't forget to drizzle the cake with a few tablespoons of brandy or liqueur before decorating.

- You might want to cover the cake with 2 lb almond paste (see page 21) before covering it with icing.

fruit and flowers

serves 24

decoration time 30 minutes

10 inch round bought or homemade
Rich Fruit Cake, covered with almond
paste (see pages 11 and 21 for
recipe and technique)

12 inch round white or red plate

confectioners' sugar or cornstarch,
for dusting

2 lb white ready-to-use icing

3 cups red fruits
(e.g., strawberries, blackberries,
clusters of red grapes, raspberries)

3 large open red roses

5 feet red ribbon, about
1½ inches wide

1 Put the cake on the plate. Dust your work surface with confectioners' sugar or cornstarch and roll out the icing to a circle, 15 inches across. Lay it over the cake, smooth the icing around the sides and trim off the excess.

2 Pile the fruits on top of the cake, starting with the larger ones and clusters of grapes.

3 Tuck the roses in among the fruits. Secure the ribbon around the sides of the cake, finishing with a bow if liked. Use a fine tea strainer to dust the fruit and flowers with confectioners' sugar.

quick tips

- One of the easiest and most effective cakes to decorate, this idea is perfect for a novice to cake decorating to practice their skills.

- The cake is ideal for a wedding anniversary, particularly a ruby wedding.

- The cake can be iced a couple of weeks in advance and the fruits and flowers added at the last minute. Make sure the fruits are dry before you arrange them on the icing, otherwise the juices will make the icing soften and the sugar dusting will dissolve.

silver wedding cake

serves 40

decoration time 1½ hours

10 inch round bought or homemade
Rich Fruit Cake, covered with almond
paste (see pages 11 and 21 for
recipe and technique)

14 inch round cake board

confectioners' sugar or cornstarch,
for dusting

2½ lb white ready-to-use icing

small 2 and 5 cutters

2 sheets or 1 small tub edible
silver leaf

5 silver or white candles

5 feet colored ribbon, about
1½ inches wide

white ribbon for edge of cake board

about 15 silver sugar coated almonds

1 Put the cake on the board. Reserve 8 oz of the icing. Dust your work surface with confectioners' sugar or cornstarch and roll out the remainder of the icing to a circle, 15 inches across. Lift the icing over the cake and smooth it around the sides, trimming off the excess around the base. Use the reserved icing to cover the cake board, trimming off the excess around the edges.

2 Thinly roll out the icing trimmings and cut out 3 each of the numbers 2 and 5. Set aside on a sheet of waxed paper.

3 Use a pair of tweezers to tear a little silver leaf from the sheet or tub. Hold it over the cake, about 2 inches away from the edge. Lightly dampen the surface of the cake where the silver is to be applied and then lower it into position, smoothing it down with a dry brush.

4 Arrange 3 number 25s on the cake, spacing them evenly apart and each about 2 inches from the edge, and fill up the areas between them with additional silver leaf. Apply more areas of silver leaf to the cake board.

5 Position the candles on top of the cake and secure the ribbon around the sides, finishing in a bow. Secure the white ribbon to the edge of the board. Scatter the sugar coated almonds in clusters over the cake and board.

quick tip

- Although silver leaf might seem difficult to use at first, you'll quickly get used to it after applying a few pieces. Because it's almost weightless, make sure you work in a draft-free area so that it doesn't blow away before you've had a chance to secure it to the cake!

golden wedding cake

serves 40

decoration time 1 hour

10 inch round bought or homemade
Rich Fruit Cake (see page 11)

7 inch round cake board

4 tablespoons smooth apricot jelly

confectioners' sugar or cornstarch,
for dusting

4 lb almond paste

12 inch round cake stand or
glass plate

4 lb white ready-to-use icing

8 feet gold ribbon,
1¼–1½ inches wide

10 gold-colored roses

plain glass tumbler, about 6 inches
tall and at least 3¼ inches
in diameter

1 Remove the cake center (see tip). Put the removed center on the cake board. Brush the top and sides of both cakes with jelly.

2 Measure the inner circumference of the ring cake with string. Dust your work surface with confectioners' sugar or cornstarch and roll out a little of the almond paste. Trim it to a strip, the length of the string and the depth of the cake. Roll up the strip and unroll it in the center of the cake, pressing it firmly in position.

3 Reserve 13 oz of the almond paste. Roll out the remainder to a circle, 15 inches across, and cut out a circle in the center, using the small dish as a template. Lift the paste over the cake so that the cut-out center lines up with the hole in the cake. Fit the paste around the sides and trim off the excess around the base. Transfer to the cake stand or plate.

4 Lightly knead the trimmings into the remaining paste and roll to a circle, 10 inches across. Lay the paste over the small cake, easing it to fit around the sides. Trim off the excess.

5 Use the white icing to cover both cakes, using the same technique as for the almond paste.

6 Secure the gold ribbon around the cakes, finishing with a bow on the bottom tier. Pour a little water into the tumbler and arrange several of the roses in it, cutting the stems to varying heights. Put it inside the ring cake. Use rose petals and more roses to decorate the tops of both cakes. Position the small cake over the glass tumbler.

quick tip

- To remove the center of the cake invert a dish with a diameter of 5 inches on the center of the cake. Holding a knife vertically, cut out the center of the cake and remove it carefully.

champagne bottle

serves 15

decoration time 1 hour

confectioners' sugar or cornstarch,
for dusting

10 oz gray ready-to-use icing

14 x 10 inch rectangular cake board

2 bought or homemade Jelly Rolls
(see page 12)

single quantity Buttercream
(see page 15)

1 lb dark green ready-to-use icing

3 oz black ready-to-use icing

2 oz white ready-to-use icing

black and gold food coloring

dark green ribbon for edges of
cake board

1 Dust your work surface with confectioners' sugar or cornstarch and thinly roll out the gray icing to a rectangle that will cover the cake board. Trim off the excess around the base.

2 Put the jelly rolls on the work surface, end to end, and cut them down to an overall length of 12 inches. Cut a "neck" out of one end, trimming off the cut edges to make a curved bottle shape. Use a little buttercream to sandwich the join in the cakes, then spread a thin layer over the cakes.

3 Roll out a little of the green icing and cut an oval, the same diameter as the base of the bottle. Press it into position. Roll out the remaining green icing and use it to cover the rest of the bottle, smoothing it to fit over the neck of the bottle and trimming off the excess around the base. Use a spatula to transfer the cake to the board, supporting it carefully under the join.

4 Roll out the black icing and use it to decorate the top of the bottle. Use the white icing and the black icing trimmings to shape the labels.

5 Use a fine paintbrush to decorate the bottle with the black and gold food colorings. Secure the ribbon around the board.

quick tip

- If you're using a bought jelly roll you might need to buy an extra one and add an additional layer because they tend to be much thinner than homemade ones.

individual
wedding cakes

makes 12

decoration time 20 minutes

12 bought or homemade Cupcakes (see page 13)

4 tablespoons sherry or orange-flavored liqueur (optional)

1½ cups confectioners' sugar, sifted

1–2 tablespoons lemon juice

36 sugar coated almonds

12 frosted flowers

fine white ribbon, to decorate

1 Drizzle the cakes with the liqueur, if using. Mix the confectioners' sugar in a bowl with 1 tablespoon of the lemon juice. Gradually add the remaining lemon juice, stirring well with a wooden spoon until the icing holds its shape but is not difficult to spread—you might not need all the juice.

2 Use a small spatula to spread the lemon-flavored icing over the tops of the cakes. Arrange 3 sugar coated almonds in the center of each cake.

3 Arrange a frosted flower on top of each cake and tie a length of white ribbon around each paper cup to decorate it, finishing with a bow.

quick tips

• To frost flowers, lightly beat an egg white in a small bowl. Put about ½ cup superfine sugar in another bowl. Either dip a flower into the egg white or use a large paintbrush to coat the petals, then sprinkle the flower generously with sugar until it is evenly coated. Transfer the flowers to a sheet of parchment paper, and leave in a cool place for at least 1 hour to dry.

• These little cakes are perfect for a country-style family wedding. You could add guests' name tags to them and place them around the dining table. Choose sugar coated almonds to suit the color scheme of the wedding. If you are using ribbon, secure it around the paper cups before you begin decorating.

4

seasonal cakes

red heart cake

serves 50–55

decoration time 1 hour

5 inch and 9 inch square bought or homemade Rich Fruit Cakes, covered with almond paste (see pages 11 and 21 for recipe and technique)

11 inch square cake board

confectioners' sugar or cornstarch, for dusting

3 lb white ready-to-use icing

heart-shaped cookie cutters in 2 or 3 sizes

6 feet red ribbon, about 1½ inches wide

red ribbon for edges of cake board

small glass dish, about 2 inches in diameter

15–20 red foil-wrapped, heart-shaped chocolates

1 Put the larger cake on the board. Dust your work surface with confectioners' sugar or cornstarch and roll out 2 lb of the icing to a 14 inch square. Lift the icing over the cake, smooth the icing down the sides and trim off the excess around the base.

2 Use the remaining icing to cover the smaller cake. Position it over the larger cake, about ¾ inch from one edge. Reserve the icing trimmings.

3 While the icing is still soft, gently press the cutters into the surface so they leave an impression when lifted away. If the cutters start to stick to the icing, dip them in a little confectioners' sugar before impressing each shape. Cover the edges of the board with the icing trimmings.

quick tips

- This cake is perfect for an unconventional wedding or a St. Valentine's Day party.

- If you use a basic sponge cake instead of rich fruit cake you do not need the layer of almond paste.

be my valentine

serves 6–8

decoration time 30 minutes,
plus chilling

**5–6 inch round bought or homemade
Rich Chocolate Cake (see page 10)**

**single quantity White Chocolate
Ganache (see page 17)**

pink, lilac, or cream-colored plate

8 oz white chocolate

pink or lilac food coloring paste

**handful of small heart-shaped
candies**

1 Cut the cake in half horizontally and sandwich the layers with a little of the ganache. Put it on the plate and spread the top and sides with the remaining ganache, swirling it in an even layer with a small spatula.

2 Measure the circumference of the cake with a piece of string. Cut a strip of waxed paper ¾ inch longer than the string and 2 inches deeper than the cake.

3 Break the chocolate into pieces and melt them in a bowl set over a pan of gently simmering water. Spoon half the chocolate onto the strip of waxed paper. Spread it to the edge of one long side and to ½ inch from both short ends. On the other long side of the strip use a thick paintbrush or pastry brush to spread the chocolate to the edges in an uneven, jagged line. Return the chocolate in the bowl to the pan, but turn off the heat so the remaining chocolate stays melted over the warm water.

4 Leave the chocolate strip to cool slightly, but do not allow it to set. Carefully wrap it around the cake (paper side outward) so that the jagged edge is uppermost. Chill for about 30 minutes until the chocolate is brittle.

5 Meanwhile, spoon 2 tablespoons of the remaining chocolate into a small bowl and beat in a dot of food coloring paste. Transfer it to a paper pastry bag and snip off the tip. Pipe about 12 heart shapes onto a sheet of waxed paper. Use a teaspoon to fill the center of each heart with the remaining chocolate, nudging it gently to the edges. Chill for 30 minutes.

6 Carefully peel away the paper from the cake. Once the chocolate hearts have set, peel away the paper and arrange the hearts on top of the cake. Scatter with the heart candies.

quick tip

- **Make sure you use food coloring paste for the decoration because liquid color will make the chocolate solidify.**

mother's day cake

serves 12

decoration time 45 minutes,
plus drying

1 egg white

⅓ cup superfine sugar

**about 25 red, pink, and
yellow primroses**

**7 inch round bought or homemade
Basic Sponge Cake (see page 9)**

½ cup lemon curd

**8 inch round or square cream-
colored plate**

**double quantity Buttercream
(see page 15)**

1 Lightly beat the egg white in a small bowl with 1 tablespoon of water until it is broken up. Put the sugar in a separate bowl. Gently pull one of the flowers away from its calyx. Using a paintbrush or your fingers, lightly coat each side of the petals in egg white. Sprinkle with superfine sugar until completely coated. Transfer the flower, face down, to a sheet of nonstick parchment paper or waxed paper. If the flower starts to fall flat, losing its shape, support it on a tiny crumpled ball of waxed paper. Frost the remaining flowers in the same way and allow them to dry for at least 1 hour or overnight.

2 Cut the cake horizontally into three and sandwich the layers together with lemon curd. Put the cake on the plate.

3 Spread a thin layer of buttercream over the top and sides of the cake to seal in the crumbs. Spread the remaining buttercream over the cake, smoothing it out with a spatula. Arrange the frosted flowers around the top edges of the cake.

quick tip

- Frosted flowers keep well for several weeks if stored in an airtight container. Make sure they're completely dry first, then arrange them in layers, interleaving each with paper towels.

chocolate egg cake

serves 10

decoration time 30 minutes

4 oz milk chocolate

8 oz dark chocolate

⅔ cup heavy cream

7 inch bought or homemade Rich Chocolate Cake (see page 10)

9–10 inch round, flat plate

selection of dark, milk, or white chocolate eggs

1 Break the milk chocolate into pieces and melt them in a bowl set over a pan of gently simmering water. Line a cookie sheet with nonstick parchment paper or waxed paper. Use a teaspoon to scribble the melted chocolate in irregular lines all over the paper. Don't try to be neat—the more casual the lines are, the better they'll be. Put the chocolate in the refrigerator for 20 minutes.

2 Chop the dark chocolate. Heat ½ cup of the cream in a small heavy saucepan until it is bubbling around the edges but not boiling. Remove from the heat and stir in the chocolate. Turn the mixture into a bowl and stir until it is melted and smooth. Stir in the remaining cream.

3 Cut the cake in half horizontally and sandwich the layers with a little of the chocolate cream. Put the cake on the plate and tip the remaining chocolate cream over the top, spreading it with a spatula so it covers the sides in swirls.

4 Take the milk chocolate shapes from the refrigerator and peel away the nonstick parchment paper or waxed paper. Break the chocolate into long, irregular pieces. Scatter them over the cake and pile the eggs on top. Keep the cake in a cool place until ready to serve.

quick tip

- If the cream boils in the pan, remove it from the heat and let it cool a little before you add the chocolate. It'll take a little longer to thicken so that it can be spread over the cake, so keep an eye on it as it cools.

easter egg

serves 8–10

preparation time 15 minutes, plus cooling

cooking time 1–1¼ hours

decoration time 30 minutes

3-egg quantity Rich Chocolate Cake (see page 10)

1¼ cups chocolate hazelnut spread

confectioners' sugar or cornstarch, for dusting

1 lb chocolate brown ready-to-use icing

2 oz milk chocolate

oval plate, about 11 inches long

5 feet ribbon, about 1½ inches wide

1 Grease a 10 cup ovenproof basin and line the base with a circle of waxed paper. Turn the cake mixture into the basin and level the surface. Bake in a preheated oven, 350°F, for 1–1¼ hours or until the cake feels just firm in the center. Leave to cool in the basin.

2 Run a knife around the edges of the basin and invert the cake on a board. To make the egg shape, start by cutting a vertical slice, 2 inches wide, off 2 opposite sides of the cake. Keeping the knife vertical, cut away more of the cake at one end to make a pointed egg shape, then round off all the edges of the cake, remembering that the cake will be shallower at the pointed end than at the thick end. Keep the trimmings. Slice the egg shape vertically into 3 layers and sandwich them together with a little of the chocolate spread. Cover the egg with the remaining chocolate spread.

3 Dust your work surface with confectioners' sugar or cornstarch and roll out the icing to an oval, 13 x 11 inches. Lift the icing over the cake and smooth it to fit around the sides. Trim off the excess around the base. Transfer the cake to a tray or board lined with nonstick parchment paper or waxed paper.

4 Break the chocolate into pieces and put them in a bowl over a pan of gently simmering water until the chocolate has melted. Put the chocolate in a paper pastry bag and snip off the tip. Using a scribbling action, pipe lines of chocolate diagonally across the egg. Use a spatula to transfer the cake to the serving plate. Keep it in a cool place until the chocolate has set.

5 Use the tip of a knife to tuck one end of the ribbon under the end of the egg. Wrap the ribbon down the length of the egg and tuck it under the other end. Use the remaining ribbon to make a large bow for the top. Secure in position with clear adhesive tape.

quick tips

- This is a perfect cake for Easter, as long as you're confident about shaping the sponge into an egg shape. Once the cake is decorated it will keep well in a cool place for several days.

- There are quite a lot of trimmings from this cake, so keep them for a trifle or mix them with melted chocolate to make truffle cakes.

a midsummer night's dream

serves 16

decoration time 1 hour

9 inch square bought or Basic Sponge Cake (see page 9)

single quantity Buttercream (see page 15)

8 tablespoons raspberry or strawberry jelly

11–12 inch square plate

confectioners' sugar or cornstarch, for dusting

2 lb lilac ready-to-use icing

8 oz dark green ready-to-use icing

8 inch square cake board

1 small set battery-operated decorative lights

small bunch of wired silk foliage

small bunch of pink, purple, or cream-colored wired silk flowers

small bunch of lavender

about 1½ lb ornamental cream-colored pebbles

1 Slice any dome off the top of the cake. Cut the cake in half horizontally and sandwich the layers with half the buttercream and all the jelly. Put the cake on the plate and spread with the remaining buttercream.

2 Dust your work surface with confectioners' sugar or cornstarch and roll out the lilac icing to a 14 inch square. Lay the icing over the cake and smooth it down the sides, trimming off the excess around the base.

3 Roll out the green icing to a 9 inch square. Lightly brush the cake board with water and lift the icing over the board. Smooth the icing over the sides and trim off the excess around the base. Reserve the trimmings. Position the board on top of the cake.

4 Put the battery-operated lights on the center of the board and position the flowers and foliage over and around the lights, making sure that the lights are evenly spaced among the flowers and that you're able to activate the switch. If necessary, use the icing trimmings to prop up the flowers on the board. Scatter the pebbles over the board to fill the gaps and conceal the batteries and wires.

quick tip

• The larger the party, the bigger you can make this cake. Whatever cake size you use, the board should be 1 inch smaller to support the decoration.

fruity celebration cake

serves 28

decoration time 45 minutes
plus chilling

**6 inch and 8 inch round bought or
homemade Rich Chocolate Cakes
(see page 10)**

10 inch round plate

**double quantity White Chocolate
Ganache (see page 17)**

12 oz white chocolate

**3 cups soft fruits
(e.g., strawberries, raspberries,
blueberries, and redcurrants)**

6 tablespoons redcurrant jelly

1 Put the larger cake on the plate. Use a spatula to spread two-thirds of the ganache over the top and sides. Position the smaller cake on top and cover it with the remaining ganache.

2 Break the chocolate into small pieces and put them in a bowl over a pan of gently simmering water. Leave until the chocolate has melted. Use a piece of string to measure the circumferences of both cakes. Cut 2 strips of waxed paper, each 1 inch longer than the circumference of the cakes and ¾ inch deeper.

3 Spread the melted chocolate over each strip of paper to within ½ inch of the ends and almost to the edges. Leave for 1–2 minutes until the chocolate has cooled slightly (but not started to set), then wrap the short strip around the small cake and the longer strip around the larger cake, paper side out.

4 Chill the cakes for about 30–60 minutes or until the chocolate is brittle, then carefully peel away the paper. Pile the fruits over the top of each cake, letting the redcurrant sprigs spill slightly over the sides.

5 To glaze the fruits, melt the redcurrant jelly with 1 tablespoon water until it is smooth. Use a pastry brush to coat the fruits evenly with the mixture.

quick tips

- For an even more intense chocolaty experience, make up an extra quantity of chocolate ganache and use it to sandwich the cakes together in 3 layers.

- An extra pair of hands will make the job of wrapping the collar of chocolate around the larger cake easier.

carnival time

serves 16

decoration time 1 hour

2 x 6 inch round bought or
homemade Basic Sponge Cakes
(see page 9)

double quantity Buttercream
(see page 15)

11–12 inch round, brightly
colored plate

confectioners' sugar or cornstarch,
for dusting

10 oz yellow ready-to-use icing

10 oz red ready-to-use icing

8 oz orange ready-to-use icing

¾ inch round cutter

selection of brightly colored
streamers or ribbons and party
poppers or tooters

1 Slice the domed surface off each cake and cut the cakes in half horizontally. Use half the buttercream to sandwich the layers together. Put one cake on top of the other, sandwiching them with a little more buttercream. Use a sharp knife to cut a "waist" out of the stacked cakes so that the stack is wider at the top and base. Put the cake on the plate and cover it with the remaining buttercream.

2 Measure the circumference at the base of the cake with a piece of string. Dust your work surface with confectioners' sugar or cornstarch and roll out 8 oz of the yellow icing to a strip the length of the string and half the overall depth of the cake. Wrap the icing around the cake, easing it to fit where the cake is narrower in the center. Roll out 8 oz of the red icing and use it to cover the top half of the cake.

3 Thinly roll out the orange icing and cut it into strips, each 1¼ inches wide. Make diagonal cuts across the strips to create large diamond shapes. Use a dampened paintbrush to secure them around the center of the cake and add halved diamond shapes around the base of the cake.

4 Roll out the remaining yellow icing and cut out plenty of small yellow circles with the cutter. Secure these to the cake, then arrange more circles on the plate. Re-roll the red icing trimmings to a circle, 6 inches across, and use it to cover the top of the cake. Pile plenty of streamers or ribbons and party poppers or tooters on top of the cake.

quick tips

- If you can't get orange icing you can make it by kneading red and yellow ready-to-use icing together.

- Buy large bags of party poppers and streamers from party and catering stores.

pumpkin patch

serves 24

decoration time 45 minutes

8 inch round bought or homemade Basic Sponge Cake (see page 9)

6 tablespoons apricot jelly

double quantity Buttercream (see page 15)

12–14 inch round wooden board

8 oz orange ready-to-use icing

confectioners' sugar or cornstarch, for dusting

½ oz chocolate brown ready-to-use icing

8 sprigs artificial foliage, each containing 3–5 leaves

1 Cut the cake in half horizontally and sandwich the layers together with the jelly and a little of the buttercream. Put the cake on the board and spread the remaining buttercream in an even layer over the top and sides, swirling it decoratively with a spatula.

2 Roll the orange icing between the palms of your hands into balls of varying sizes, dusting your hands with confectioners' sugar or cornstarch if the icing starts to stick. Flatten each ball lightly into a pumpkin shape and make deep grooves evenly all around the sides of the pumpkins with the back of a knife.

3 Roll the brown icing into a rope and cut it into short lengths. Dampen one end of each length with a paintbrush and secure them to the pumpkins for the stalks.

4 Arrange some of the foliage on top of the cake, nestling all but one of the pumpkins among the leaves. Arrange more leaves and the remaining pumpkin around the base of the cake.

quick tip

• The little pumpkins on this cake are surprisingly easy to make and look stunning nestling in their green leaves. They'll look even more effective if they're all different sizes, so don't be too precise.

spider's web

serves 16

decoration time 30 minutes

8 inch round bought or homemade
Basic Sponge Cake (see page 9)

double quantity Buttercream
(see page 15)

13–14 inch round plate, preferably
red or orange

confectioners' sugar or cornstarch,
for dusting

2 lb white ready-to-use icing

1 tube black decorator frosting

black food coloring

½ oz black ready-to-use icing

1 flat licorice bootlace

several gummy snakes or insects

orange or black candles

1 Cut the cake in half horizontally and sandwich the layers together with half the buttercream. Put the cake on the plate and spread over the remaining buttercream.

2 Dust your work surface with confectioners' sugar or cornstarch and roll out about 1¾ lb of the white icing to a circle, 13 inches across. Lay the icing over the cake and smooth it around the sides, trimming off the excess icing around the base.

3 Use the black decorator frosting to pipe 6 lines over the top of the cake, crossing them in the center. Working from the center outward, pipe curved lines of icing to resemble a spider's web.

4 Roll 2 oz of the reserved white icing into a ball, then mold it into a ghost shape. Press the shape onto the surface to make sure it stands upright, then secure it to one side of the web with a dampened paintbrush. Paint the ghost's eyes and mouth with the black food coloring using a fine brush.

5 Make the spider. Roll the black icing into a ball and position it on the web. Cut 8 pieces of licorice, each 1½ inches long, and secure 4 on either side of the black icing ball. Arrange a few gummy snakes or insects on the web.

6 Roll the remaining white icing into a long, thin rope and arrange it in a curvy line around the sides of the cake. Push the candles into the icing for support.

quick tip

• Using a tube of icing to create the web is much easier than it looks, but there will be enough icing in the tube to pipe a web on a plate if you want to practice first.

haunted house

serves 15

decoration time 30 minutes

5 oz luxury dark or milk
cooking chocolate

12 inch bought chocolate jelly roll

6 inch bought chocolate jelly roll

9 inch round cake board

3 ice cream cones

8 oz milk chocolate buttons

4 oz white ready-to-use icing

brown paste food coloring

confectioners' sugar or cornstarch,
for dusting

2 teaspoons smooth apricot jelly

1 tube black decorator frosting

Halloween candles and
candle-holders

1 Break the chocolate into pieces and put them into a large, heatproof bowl set over a saucepan of simmering water. Leave until just melted. Meanwhile, cut one-third off the large jelly roll.

2 Spread a thin layer of melted chocolate over the cake board and stand all the jelly roll pieces up on their ends so that they touch each other and resemble a castle, with the shortest piece of jelly roll at the front.

3 Spread melted chocolate over the ice cream cones and stick them to the top of the jelly rolls with a little more chocolate. Press chocolate buttons in overlapping rows over the cones to resemble roof tiles, beginning at the widest part of the cone and working upward, adding extra chocolate to the back of the buttons as you near the tip of the cones.

4 Reserve half the white icing and color the remainder light brown. Dust your work surface with confectioners' sugar or cornstarch and roll out the icing. Cut out windows, windowsills, and a double door. Stick them onto the cake with a little apricot jelly and use a small knife to mark the door with lines. Add two tiny balls of icing for doorknobs.

5 Knead and roll out the white icing. Cut out ghost shapes and stick them to the windows with a little jelly. Add tiny white balls for eyes and pipe black eyes and mouths with decorator frosting. Arrange the candles and candle-holders on the cake board.

quick tips

- If you find that some of the chocolate buttons slide off the chocolate-covered ice cream cones, position just 2–3 rows on each cone to start with, then gradually add extra layers as the chocolate begins to set, sticking them on with more melted chocolate.

- If you are planning to transport the cake to a party, secure the cakes with long wooden testers inserted through the centers of the ice cream cones, so the tops of the turrets don't topple over in transit, adding sticks at step 2.

fireworks cake

serves 12

preparation time 10 minutes

cooking time about 50 minutes

decoration time 1 hour, plus drying

confectioners' sugar or cornstarch,
for dusting

4 oz yellow ready-to-use icing

2 inch and 1¼ inch star cutters

8 oz orange ready-to-use icing

4 oz red ready-to-use icing

20 lengths heavy gauge floral wire,
cut to various lengths

4-egg quantity Basic Sponge Cake
mixture (see page 9)

double quantity Buttercream
(see page 15)

8 inch square plate

1 lb dark blue ready-to-use icing

1 Dust your work surface with confectioners' sugar or cornstarch and roll out three-quarters of the yellow icing. Cut out stars in both sizes. Roll out a third of the orange icing and cut out more stars. Lightly dampen some of the large yellow stars with water and secure some of the small orange stars to them. Bend the tip of a length of floral wire over to create a hook and push it into the center of a star. Repeat with the other stars. Cut out more shapes, such as "wheels" of red and yellow icing and long, ribbony shapes, and thread these onto more wires. Transfer all the shapes to a large cookie sheet lined with nonstick parchment paper and leave them to harden for several hours, preferably overnight. Reserve the icing trimmings.

2 Turn the cake mixture into a greased and lined pan, 10 inches square, and level the surface. Bake in a preheated oven, 325°F, for about 50 minutes until just firm and a tester, inserted into the center, comes out clean. Allow to cool.

3 Slice the dome off the top of the cake and cut it into 4 equal pieces. Sandwich the cakes into a stack with half the buttercream and transfer to the plate. Spread the remaining buttercream over the top and sides.

4 Roll out more orange icing and cut out a 5 inch square. Put this on top of the cake. Roll out the blue icing and cut out 4 squares to cover the sides. Position these around the cake, pressing them together at the corners to seal. Use strips of the remaining orange icing to decorate the top and bottom edges.

5 Use the red and yellow icing trimmings to cut out ribbon and star shapes. Secure these around the box. Press the wired shapes into the top of the cake to finish.

quick tip

- Floral wire can be easily bent to form small hooks with small pliers. It's sold in pre-cut packs or in rolls.

candied fruit cake

serves 24

decoration time 30 minutes

8 inch round bought or homemade
Rich Fruit Cake (see page 11)

6 tablespoons smooth apricot jelly

3 tablespoons brandy

confectioners' sugar or cornstarch,
for dusting

1 lb yellow or white almond paste

10 inch round serving plate

8 oz selection of crystallized fruits
(e.g., cherries, papaya, mango,
melon, pineapple)

4–5 dates, halved and pitted

3–5 feet orange ribbon,
2 inches wide

1 Put the cake on a cookie sheet. Blend the jelly with the brandy and spread a little over the sides of the cake.

2 Measure the circumference of the cake with a piece of string. Dust your work surface with confectioners' sugar or cornstarch and roll out three-quarters of the almond paste to a strip the length of the string and ½ inch deeper than the cake. Secure the strip around the cake.

3 Halve the remaining almond paste and roll out each piece to a long, thin rope, slightly shorter than the string. Twist the 2 ropes together and arrange the twist around the top edge of the cake. Put the cake under a moderate broiler for 2–3 minutes, watching the paste closely until it is evenly toasted. (Rotate the cookie sheet slightly to get an even color.)

4 Transfer the cake to a serving plate. Cut all the fruits into equal pieces. Brush the top of the cake with a little more glaze and scatter over the fruits. Brush the fruits with the remaining glaze and secure the ribbon around the sides.

quick tip

• This cake is a perfect choice for marzipan lovers or those who find icing just too sweet. You can buy mixed bags of candied fruits, including pineapple, papaya, and mango, to which you can add some candied cherries. Boxes of whole candied fruits are also available—although they are rather expensive—from gourmet stores. These can be cut into large pieces so that the shape of the fruit is still recognizable.

christmas star

serves 12

decoration time about 1 hour, plus drying

confectioners' sugar or cornstarch, for dusting

2½ lb white ready-to-use icing

2 inch and 1¼ inch star cutters

10 inch round bought or homemade Basic Sponge Cake (see page 9)

double quantity Buttercream (see page 15)

4 tablespoons smooth raspberry or strawberry jelly

11 inch round cake board

selection of silver and gold balls

silver or gold food coloring

ribbon for edge of cake board

1 Dust your work surface with confectioners' sugar or cornstarch and thinly roll out 4 oz of the icing. Use the larger cutter to cut out plenty of star shapes. Cut out the center of each star with the small cutter and transfer the stars to a lined cookie sheet. Leave for several hours or overnight.

2 Cut out a circle of paper, 10 inches across, and fold it in half. Fold the halved paper into three to make a wedge 6 sheets thick. Make a pencil mark 2 inches from the point and an equal distance from the sides. Draw a line from each outer corner to the pencil mark. Cut along the lines and open out the paper into a star. Rest the star over the cake and use it as a template for cutting out a star shape. Cut the cake in half horizontally and sandwich with half the buttercream and all the jelly. Spread the remaining buttercream over the cake.

3 Thinly roll out a further 9 oz of the icing and use it to cover the cake board, trimming off and reserving the excess around the base.

4 Lift the cake onto the board. Roll out half the remaining icing and cut out long strips, each the depth of the cake. Use these to cover the sides of the cake, pushing the strips well into the corners and emphasizing the star shape by pinching the icing into points. Work in manageable strips of icing.

5 Roll out the remaining icing to a circle, 10 inches across, and use the paper template to cut out a star. Dampen the top edges of the icing around the sides and lift the star onto the cake, pressing the icing together around the edges.

6 Press the silver and gold balls into the top and sides of the cake and over the board. If necessary, dampen the icing with a fine paintbrush to help them stick. Paint the star shapes and arrange them on the cake. Secure the ribbon around the edge of the cake board.

quick tips

- Freeze the sponge trimmings from the cake and use them in a Christmas trifle.

- If you find shaping the cake difficult, you might be able to buy, or hire, a star-shaped cake cutter, in which case you might prefer to use a rich fruit cake mixture instead of a sponge cake.

jagged jewel cake

serves 24

decoration time 20 minutes

8 inch round bought or homemade
Rich Fruit Cake, covered with almond
paste (see pages 11 and 21 for
recipe and technique)

10–12 inch round glass plate,
preferably red

confectioners' sugar or cornstarch,
for dusting

2 lb white ready-to-use icing

8 oz red, purple, orange, and green
clear hard candies

6 red tea lights

36 inches red ribbon, about
1½ inches wide

1 Put the cake on the plate. Dust your work surface with confectioners' sugar or cornstarch and roll out the icing to a circle, 13 inches across. Lay it over the cake, smoothing the icing around the sides and trimming off the excess around the base.

2 Line a large cookie sheet with kitchen foil. Unwrap the candies and space them about 1½ inches apart on the foil, making sure the colors are evenly mixed. Put the candies in a preheated oven, 400°F, for 3–5 minutes until they have melted together and are bubbling but not turning brown. Watch closely for the last couple of minutes because the candies will quickly darken and start to burn. Leave them to cool on the foil.

3 Peel away the foil from the candies and use your fingers to break the candies into large, jagged pieces.

4 Arrange the tea lights in a circle in the center of the cake. Surround these with the sweet brittle, pushing the pieces gently into the icing. Tie the ribbon around the cake and light the candles just before serving.

quick tip

• The candies can be melted up to 2 days in advance. Once they have cooled, leave them on the foil-lined cookie sheet and cover tightly with lightly greased plastic wrap. This will stop them softening and turning sticky. Once they are on the cake, the candies should stay brittle for a couple of days before they begin to soften.

citrus candle cake

serves 40

decoration time 30 minutes

10 inch round bought or homemade Rich Fruit Cake, covered with almond paste (see pages 11 and 21 for recipe and technique)

12 inch round glass plate

double quantity Royal Icing (see page 18)

5 small clementines

5 tea lights

several small sprigs of bay leaves

5 cinnamon sticks

12 gold dragées

3–5 feet gold-edged ribbon, about 1¼ inches wide

1 Put the cake on the plate. Cover it with the icing, swirling it over the top and sides with a spatula.

2 Cut a slice off the top of each clementine and scoop out as much flesh as possible. Dry the clementine skins on paper towels. The flesh sometimes comes away cleanly, leaving dry skins, in which case you won't need to dry them.

3 Put a tea light inside each clementine and arrange them around the top of the cake. Tuck the sprigs of bay leaves, the cinnamon sticks, and dragées between the fruits.

4 Tie the ribbon around the sides of the cake, finishing with a bow, if desired.

quick tip

- You can cover a cake with royal icing up to 2 weeks in advance, but leave the clementines and other decoration until the day before you want to serve the cake so that they don't deteriorate.

easter chicks

makes 8

decoration time 25 minutes

8 bought or homemade Cupcakes (see page 13)

double quantity citrus Buttercream, colored yellow (see page 15)

confectioners' sugar or cornstarch, for dusting

8 oz yellow ready-to-use icing

4 oz orange ready-to-use icing

16 edible silver balls

1 Remove the paper cups, spear each cake with a fork and spread the tops and sides thickly with buttercream.

2 Dust your work surface with confectioners' sugar or cornstarch and knead the yellow ready-to-use icing. Shape 8 small balls from some of the icing and stick them to the cakes for chick heads. Dot the tops with a little buttercream.

3 Roll out the remaining yellow icing and stamp out eight 2 inch rounds with a plain cookie cutter, re-rolling the trimmings as necessary. Cut the rounds in half and mark the edges with a small knife to resemble feathers. Press them to the sides of the chicks.

4 Shape tiny triangles of orange icing and stick them to the chick heads with a little water for beaks. Roll the remainder into thin ropes and cut into 16 x 2 inch lengths. Make 2 slits in the end of each "leg" piece for feet and then stick the chick bodies onto the legs with any remaining buttercream. Add the edible silver balls for eyes. Arrange on a plate or cake board.

quick tips

- If you can't buy ready-colored icing, mix white ready-to-use icing with a little red and yellow paste colorings to make orange.

- Ready-made muffins could also be used, but, as they are a little larger, you will have only enough buttercream for the chicks. If you have tiny children, you could also make mini-versions with cakes or muffins made in petit four cups.

easter nests

makes 12

decoration time 20 minutes

single quantity chocolate
Buttercream (see page 15) or
Chocolate Fudge Frosting
(see page 18)

12 bought or homemade chocolate
Cupcakes (see page 13)

8 oz flaked chocolate bars, cut into
1 inch lengths

36 covered chocolate mini-eggs

1 Use a small spatula to spread the buttercream or chocolate frosting over the tops of the cakes, spreading the mixture right to the edges.

2 Cut the short lengths of flaked chocolate bars lengthwise into thin shards.

3 Arrange the chocolate shards around the edges of the cakes, pressing them into the icing at different angles to resemble birds' nests. Pile 3 eggs into the center of each "nest."

quick tip

• Cutting chocolate flake can be extremely messy. Use chocolate sprinkles instead.

duck, bunny, and chick

makes 12

decoration time 25 minutes

single quantity Buttercream
(see page 15)

yellow and blue food colorings

12 bought or homemade Cupcakes
(see page 13)

2 candied cherries

1 Put two-thirds of the buttercream in a bowl, beat in a few drops of yellow food coloring and mix well. Use a small spatula to spread it in an even layer over the tops of the cakes.

2 Color the remaining buttercream with blue food coloring. Transfer it to a pastry bag fitted with a writing tip or use a waxed paper pastry bag with the tip snipped off.

3 Pipe simple duck, bunny, and chick shapes on to the iced cakes. Cut the candied cherries into thin slices, then into tiny triangles and use them to represent beaks on the ducks and chicks, and tiny eyes on the bunnies.

quick tip

• Specialty cooking stores will stock cookie cutters in the shape of animals and birds, which you could use to cut shapes from rolled-out colored icing. Decorate them with candied cherries or paint on features with food coloring and a paintbrush or decorator frosting.

flying bats

makes 12

decoration time 30 minutes

**confectioners' sugar or cornstarch,
for dusting**

4 oz black ready-to-use icing

2 tablespoons honey

**12 bought or homemade Cupcakes
(see page 13)**

6 oz orange ready-to-use icing

1 tube black decorator frosting

**selection of tiny red, orange, and
yellow candies**

1 Dust your work surface with confectioners' sugar or cornstarch and knead the black ready-to-use icing. Roll it out thickly and cut out 12 bat shapes by hand or using a small bat-shaped cookie cutter. Transfer to a cookie sheet lined with nonstick parchment paper and allow to harden while you decorate the cakes.

2 Spread ½ teaspoon honey over the top of each cake. Thinly roll out the orange ready-to-use icing and cut out circles with a plain 2½ inch cookie cutter. Arrange an orange circle on top of each cake.

3 Put a bat on top of each cake. Pipe a wiggly line of black icing around the edge of the cake. Dampen the edge of the orange icing and press the candies gently over the black icing.

quick tips

- If you're making these cakes for a Halloween party, you could decorate them with black cats or witches' hats and broomsticks.

- Decorate the table with plastic Halloween figures or foil ghosts, pumpkins, bats, and other scary shapes, all of which are available from specialty party stores.

wicked witches

makes 4

decoration time 20 minutes

4 ice cream cones

3 oz dark or milk luxury cooking chocolate

4 chocolate-covered or plain graham crackers

single quantity green Buttercream (see page 15)

4 bought chocolate-chip muffins

2 oz red strawberry-flavored bootlaces

4 small different-colored soft candies

4 different-colored gummy candies

1 tube black decorator frosting

13 x 5 inch green cake board

1 Trim the curved tops off the ice cream cones with a serrated knife and discard them.

2 Break the chocolate into pieces and melt them in a bowl set over a pan of gently simmering water. Spread a little melted chocolate over each cracker, then spread the remainder over the outside of the ice cream cones. Stick the cones onto the crackers to make the witches' hats and leave for 5 minutes to set.

3 Spread buttercream over the muffins. Cut the bootlaces into 5–6 inch lengths and press them onto the muffins for hair. Halve the small soft candies, attach them to the muffin faces for eyes. Stick on gummy sweet noses and pipe on black eyebrows and jagged, angry mouths.

4 Dot the remaining buttercream on top of the bootlace "hair" and stick the hats in place. Arrange the witches on a cake board or plate to serve.

quick tips

- Make these witches look even more sinister by serving them on a black china plate, a cake board covered with black paper, or a black marble cheese board.

- Hats, hair, and facial features can be added to scoops of vanilla or strawberry ice cream instead of muffins.

eyeballs

makes 8

decoration time 25 minutes

8 bought or homemade Cupcakes (see page 13)

3 tablespoons smooth apricot jelly

confectioners' sugar or cornstarch, for dusting

1 lb white ready-to-use icing

4 green candied cherries, halved

4 yellow candied cherries, halved

2 black licorice twists

red paste food coloring

1 If necessary, trim the tops of the cakes to level them. Brush the tops and sides of cakes with jelly.

2 Dust your work surface with confectioners' sugar or cornstarch, knead the icing and cut it into 7 pieces. Thinly roll out a piece until it is a little larger than a cake. Drape it over a cake, smooth the top and sides and pinch each side to form an eye shape. Trim off the excess and reserve.

3 Repeat until all the cakes are covered, re-kneading the icing trimmings to cover the final cake. Press a halved cherry into the top of each cake for the iris and add a thin slice of licorice for the pupil.

4 Put a little red coloring onto a saucer, add a drop of water and mix together. Use a fine paintbrush to paint blood vessels on the top of each eyeball. Arrange the cakes on a cake board or plate to serve.

quick tips

• This idea can be adapted by shaping a little white icing around halved green seedless grapes instead of the candied cherries. Add a little licorice for the pupil.

• If you are making your own cakes, add your child's favorite flavoring.

pumpkin lanterns

makes 6

decoration time 30 minutes

12 bought or homemade Cupcakes (see page 13)

½ quantity vanilla Buttercream (see page 15)

1¼ lb white ready-to-use icing

yellow and red paste food colorings

confectioners' sugar or cornstarch, for dusting

1 teaspoon smooth apricot jelly

1 If necessary, trim the tops of the cakes to level them. Sandwich the cake tops together with buttercream, then spread the remaining buttercream thinly over the sides and bases of the cakes.

2 Color 2 oz of the ready-to-use icing yellow and wrap it in plastic wrap. Color the remainder orange using a little yellow and red paste food coloring. Dust your work surface with confectioners' sugar or cornstarch and knead the icing well.

3 Cut the orange icing into 5 pieces. Thinly roll out a piece, then put a cake pair on it so that the joins of the cake are vertical. Pleat the edges of the icing up and over the cakes and trim off any excess. Smooth the icing edges with sugar if necessary. Continue covering the cakes in the same way, re-rolling the trimmings to cover the final cake.

4 Thinly roll out the yellow icing and cut triangular eye shapes and jagged mouths. Stick them to the cakes with a little apricot jelly. Mix the yellow trimmings with any orange trimmings and shape them into a thick rope. Mark the sides with a knife, then slice and stick the rope to the tops of the lanterns for pumpkin stalks. Arrange on a cake board or plate to serve.

quick tips

• If your cake board is a little battered or scratched, cover it with colored foil or with thinly rolled out dark green ready-to-use icing. Trim the icing flush with the edge of the cake board, then shape the trimmings into thin ropes and twist them between the pumpkin lanterns, adding leaves if desired.

• Small individual cakes can be transformed into ghostly cakes by sandwiching two together and draping them with large circles of rolled-out white ready-to-use icing so that it falls in soft folds. Pipe on black eyes and jagged mouths.

christmas reindeer

serves 12

decoration time 25 minutes

12 x 9 x 2 inch homemade Rich Chocolate Cake (see page 10)

16 x 12 inch rectangular cake board

double quantity chocolate Buttercream (see page 15)

confectioners' sugar or cornstarch, for dusting

4 oz light brown ready-to-use icing

1½ oz red ready-to-use icing

½ oz white ready-to-use icing

chocolate sticks

sifted confectioners' sugar, to serve

1 Put the cake on a cutting board and cut it in half to make 2 rectangles, each 9 x 6 inches. Cut one of these halves in half again to make 2 rectangles, each 6 x 4½ inches. Finally, cut one of the smaller pieces into 3 strips, each 4½ x 2 inches.

2 Arrange the largest piece of cake on the cake board for the reindeer body, cutting off the corners to make a curved shape. Use the next largest piece for the head and cut off the corners to make a curved shape. Overlap the head and body and tuck the cake trimmings under the top of the head to support it.

3 Use two of the smaller pieces to make the legs, cutting the tops at a slight angle so that the legs are not completely upright. Use the remaining piece of cake to lengthen the reindeer's head.

4 Stick the cut edges of the cake together with buttercream, where necessary, then use the rest to cover the top and sides of the cake. Wipe any excess icing off the board with paper towels.

5 Dust your work surface with confectioners' sugar or cornstarch and knead the light brown ready-to-use icing. Roll out a little and use it to cover the ends of the legs to make hooves. Trim off the excess. Roll out the remaining light brown icing and cut oval ears, about 3 inches long, and a smiling mouth. Put them on the cake, pinching the ends of the ears together.

6 Shape the red icing into a ball and put it on the head for the nose. Shape the white icing into 2 ovals, and press them onto the head for eyes, sticking on small pieces of chocolate stick for eyeballs. Add whole and halved pieces of chocolate sticks for antlers. Shield the cake with a piece of paper and dust the cake board with sifted confectioners' sugar just before serving.

quick tips

- If you don't want to open a large pack of white ready-to-use icing just to the make the eyes, use 2 white chocolate buttons instead.

- Because the amounts of ready-to-use icing required are so small, you might prefer to divide and color a pack of white icing.

father christmas faces

makes 12

decoration time 20 minutes

12 bought or homemade Cupcakes(see page 13)

single quantity plain Buttercream (see page 15)

4 oz luxury white chocolate, coarsely grated

24 dried cranberries

24 sugar-coated chocolate chips or small covered chocolate drops

confectioners' sugar or cornstarch, for dusting

4 oz red ready-to-use icing

1 tube red decorator frosting

1 If necessary, trim the tops off the cakes to level them, then spread them with buttercream. Holding each cake over a plate, sprinkle with the grated white chocolate. Put it on a serving plate or cake board.

2 Press cranberry cheeks and chocolate-drop eyes onto the cakes.

3 Dust your work surface with confectioners' sugar or cornstarch and knead the ready-to-use icing. Roll it out thinly and cut triangles, about 2 inches long, and press them onto the tops of the cakes, sticking them with a little more buttercream and curling the tops slightly.

4 Pipe on red mouths with decorator frosting.

quick tip

• **To turn an everyday tea into a special occasion, keep a handy supply of homemade cupcakes in the freezer and decorate them while they are still frozen.**

snowy cupcakes

makes 12

decoration time 20 minutes,
plus drying

confectioners' sugar or cornstarch,
for dusting

2 oz white ready-to-use icing

1¼ inch star cutter

1½ cups confectioners' sugar

2 tablespoons lemon juice

12 bought or homemade Cupcakes
(see page 13)

⅔ cup shredded coconut

1 Dust your work surface with confectioners' sugar or cornstarch and roll out the icing. Cut out 12 stars. Transfer them to a cookie sheet lined with nonstick parchment paper or waxed paper and leave them to harden for at least 1 hour.

2 Beat the confectioners' sugar in a bowl with 1 tablespoon lemon juice. Gradually add the remaining juice until the icing just holds its shape but is not too thick to spread. You might not need all the lemon juice.

3 Use a small spatula to spread the icing over the cakes. Sprinkle plenty of shredded coconut over each cake and gently press a star shape into the top.

quick tips

• These little cakes make a lovely gift, particularly if you put them in a shallow, square box, tied with a stunning ribbon.

• These cakes couldn't be easier to decorate and are best made up to a day in advance so they're perfectly fresh when you present them to your guests.

christmas garland

makes 1 garland of 24 cakes

decoration time 15 minutes

6 tablespoons apricot jelly

1 tablespoon water

24 bought fruit and nut or cranberry cupcakes

confectioners' sugar, for dusting

bunch of red grapes, washed

bunch of green grapes, washed

3–4 clementines, halved

3–4 figs, halved

plenty of bay leaf sprigs

1 Press the jelly through a strainer into a small saucepan and add the water. Heat gently until softened then spread in a thin layer over the tops of the cakes.

2 Arrange 15–16 of the cakes in a staggered circle on a round flat plate or tray, at least 14 inches in diameter. Use a fine sifter or tea strainer to dust the cakes on the plate with plenty of confectioners' sugar.

3 Fold a piece of paper into 4 thicknesses then cut out a holly leaf shape, about 2½ inches long. Press a holly leaf paper template gently on the center of 4 more cakes and dust lavishly with confectioners' sugar. Carefully lift off the templates by sliding a knife under the paper to remove them without disturbing the confectioners' sugar. Repeat on the remaining cakes. Arrange the cakes in a circle on top of the first layer.

4 Cut the grapes into small clusters. Tuck all the fruits into the gaps around the cakes and into the center of the plate. Finish by arranging small sprigs of bay leaves around the fruits.

quick tip

• For extra decorative effect, use gold, silver, patterned, or white paper bake cups.

Index

acknowledgments

Executive Editor: Sarah Ford

Project Editor: Kate Tuckett

Executive Art Editor: Joanna MacGregor

Designer: Ginny Zeal

Production Controller: Nigel Reed

picture acknowledgments

Alamy/Adrian Franklin 11.

Octopus Publishing Group Limited/David Jordan 4 left, 7 left, 7 right, 16 right, 20 right, 24 top left, 24 top right, 24 bottom right, 24 bottom left, 27, 29, 31, 33, 35, 37, 39, 41, 43, 45, 47, 49, 51, 53, 63, 65, 67, 71, 75, 77, 166 top right, 166 bottom right, 189, 201, 209, 211, 213, 215, 217; /Lis Parsons 1, 2-3, 8 left, 8 right, 14, 15 top, 16 left, 17 top, 17 bottom, 18 top, 18 bottom, 19, 20 left, 21 top right, 21 bottom left, 22 left, 22 right, 23 left, 23 right, 55, 57, 59, 82 top left, 82 top right, 82 bottom left, 85, 87, 89, 91, 93, 95, 97, 99, 101, 103, 105, 107, 109, 111, 113, 130 top left, 130 top right, 130 bottom left, 133, 135, 136, 139, 141, 143, 145, 147, 149, 151, 153, 155, 157, 159, 161, 163, 166 top left, 169, 171, 173, 175, 177, 179, 181, 183, 185, 187, 191, 193, 195, 197, 199, 219; /William Reavell 10; /Gareth Sambidge 4 right, 5, 6, 13, 15 bottom, 61, 69, 73, 79, 81, 82 bottom right, 115, 117, 119, 121, 123, 125, 127, 129, 130 bottom right, 165, 166 bottom left, 203, 205, 207, 221; /Simon Smith 12.